To Phil Walker,
with best wishes
for the future.

[signature]

March 23, 2009

"To Bear Any Burden":

A Hoosier Green Beret's
Letters from Vietnam

Captain Daniel H. FitzGibbon at Special Forces Camp Ha Tay, 1968.
Daniel H. FitzGibbon

"To Bear Any Burden":

A Hoosier Green Beret's Letters from Vietnam

Daniel H. FitzGibbon

Foreword by David L. Anderson

Indiana Historical Society Press
Indianapolis 2005

Printed in the United States of America

This book is a publication of the
Indiana Historical Society Press
450 West Ohio Street
Indianapolis, Indiana 46202-3269 USA
www.indianahistory.org

Telephone orders 1-800-447-1830
Fax orders 317-234-0562
Orders by e-mail shop@indianahistory.org

The paper in this publication meets the minimum requirements of American National Standard for Information Sciences—Permanence of Paper for Printed Library Materials, ANSI Z39.48-1984. ∞

Library of Congress Cataloging-in-Publication Data

FitzGibbon, Daniel H.
  To bear any burden : a Hoosier Green Beret's letters from Vietnam / Daniel H. FitzGibbon ; foreword by David L. Anderson.
      p. cm.
  ISBN 0-87195-179-7 (alk. paper)
  1. Vietnamese Conflict, 1961-1975—Personal narratives, American. 2. FitzGibbon, Daniel H.—Correspondence. I. Title.

DS559.5.F535 2005
959.704'342'092—dc22

                                        2004065768

To all veterans of the Fifth Special Forces Group (Airborne) in Vietnam, living and dead, with deep respect, admiration, and pride.
De Oppressor Liber.

CONTENTS

Foreword. ix

Preface xxiii

Introduction 1

Letters 9

Epilogue. 127

Glossary 139

Daniel H. FitzGibbon as a cadet at West Point, 1961.
Daniel H. FitzGibbon

FOREWORD

Military Courage and Common Sense

David L. Anderson

Courage and common sense were abundant and often overlooked qualities among the more than two and half million American men and women who served in the U.S. armed forces in South Vietnam during the Vietnam War. The letters that you are about to read were written during the war by Captain Daniel H. FitzGibbon, U.S. Army, who was one of those Americans. As are most letters, these were written for an immediate purpose—to keep his family informed of what he was doing and that he was alright—and they were not intended to be a historical record. As read now, however, they document one soldier's earnest efforts to do his duty with honor and effectiveness. In the process, the letters provide significant insights into one of the major public policy failures in American history. Because they are letters and not essays, they argue no particular interpretation of U.S. policy in Vietnam, but they are articulate and perceptive descriptions of some of the most salient issues that have been raised about the American conduct of the war.

Born in Columbus, Indiana, FitzGibbon graduated from the U.S. Military Academy at West Point in 1964. After being stationed in West Berlin, Germany, he went to Vietnam in February 1968 as a member of the U.S. Army Special Forces or Green Berets, as they were called because of their distinctive headgear. Having graduated from West Point and gone through the rigorous training at the Special Forces School at Fort Bragg, North Carolina, FitzGibbon was not an average soldier but was one of an elite group considered to be among the best the army had. Even within those ranks he stood out for special recognition. His career and actions were not typical, but there really was no typical experience for Americans in Vietnam. There are almost as many variations in Vietnam War narratives as there are Vietnam veterans. The perception of the war and the meaning of the experience depended a great deal upon when a person was in Vietnam, where he or she served, and what his or her particular duty assignment was. For FitzGibbon the time was 1968, the place was north-central Vietnam (known to the military as II Corps), and the assignment was counterinsurgency warfare.

FitzGibbon arrived in South Vietnam at the army's huge Cam Ranh Bay replacement center on February 6, 1968, and then proceeded to the Fifth Special Forces Group headquarters at Nha Trang to receive his specific orders. It was only a week after the forces of the communist-led National Liberation Front, which South Vietnamese government officials and most Americans referred to as the Vietcong or Vietnamese Communists, had begun the Tet Offensive. Tet is the lunar New Year, and during this most festive of all Vietnamese holidays, the Vietcong—supported by elements of the North Vietnamese Army (NVA)—had simultaneously attacked the major cities and towns throughout South Vietnam and many U.S. and Army of the Republic of Vietnam (ARVN) military installations. The purpose was to break the military stalemate that had developed and to try to ignite a popular uprising against the American-backed Republic of Vietnam (RVN). American and ARVN units repulsed most of these assaults after several days of heavy fighting, and no uprising began.

The ability of the communist forces to strike such a significant and surprising blow after three years of U.S. military pressure on them created serious doubt, however, about the entire American war effort. Influential voices in Congress and the news media

**Black smoke hovers over a street in Saigon, South Vietnam,
as fire trucks rush to scenes of fires during attacks by Vietcong
during the Tet Offensive.**
Time Life Pictures/Getty Images

joined already growing expressions of antiwar sentiment to urge President Lyndon B. Johnson to halt further escalation of American involvement and to accept a negotiated settlement with North Vietnam. In retrospect, it can be seen that the Tet Offensive and the reassessment of the strategic value of Vietnam to the United States that it started were the beginning of a political process that ended Johnson's presidency, divided the Democratic Party, helped elect Republican Richard Nixon as president, and finally resulted in a gradual de-escalation of American military involvement in Vietnam.

For the more than 500,000 U.S. soldiers who were in South Vietnam with FitzGibbon, however, the war did not seem to be coming to an end but rather to be locked in an even more violent stalemate. The total of U.S. military personnel killed in Vietnam in 1968 was 14,589, which represented 25 percent of all Americans killed during the war. In Washington on March 31, Johnson announced a limitation of U.S. bombing of North Vietnam, a readiness to begin negotiations, and his own withdrawal as a candidate for reelection. Meetings began in Paris on May 13 between American and North Vietnamese diplomats, but it was clear that both sides intended to continue fighting while talking. The usually hard to find main force Vietcong military units had exposed themselves in the Tet Offensive and suffered extensive losses in the U.S. and ARVN counterattacks. Hanoi made concerted efforts to infiltrate reinforcements and matériel into the South along the Ho Chi Minh Trail that went from the North through Laos and Cambodia into the RVN. American military commanders were equally determined to disrupt this infiltration and prevent any repetition of the January–February enemy offensive. In a so-called Mini-Tet Offensive in May, another round of intense combat occurred in I Corps, the five provinces of South Vietnam just south of the demilitarized zone that divided the two Vietnams, and again U.S. and ARVN units withstood the assault.

As the fighting intensified in I Corps, FitzGibbon was in command of a Special Forces A-Team camp at Ha Tay about fifty miles north of Qui Nhon in II Corps, which was the military term for a vast area stretching north from Saigon about 400 miles. II Corps contained some major combat bases, such as Cam Ranh Bay and Nha Trang, and a densely populated coastal lowland, but most of II Corps was the Central Highlands, a sparsely populated mountainous region that included the Cambodian border on its west side. The Ho Chi Minh Trail entered into the Central Highlands at several points, and the remote, undeveloped mountain ridges and valleys provided well-hidden base areas for the NVA and the Vietcong regular forces. Both sides in the war considered the Central Highlands to be one of the most critical areas in South Vietnam, and the region was the location of many major battles and operations. In 1968 the U.S. Army had brigades of its Fourth Infantry Division stationed at various times at Pleiku, Dak To, Kontum, and Ban Me Thuot; its 173rd Airborne Brigade located at Bong Son; and more than fifty Special Forces camps at locations throughout the Central Highlands. In September 1968 the Special Forces reached its highest strength during the war with 3,542 assigned personnel throughout all of South Vietnam.

A military concept with a long tradition, the modern Special Forces came into existence in the 1950s as elite troops who were experts in unconventional warfare operations behind enemy lines. Put through a highly competitive selection and arduous training process, these soldiers had to be airborne qualified and proficient in multiple skills, including survival, sabotage, weaponry, medicine, communications, intelligence gathering, and languages. As the American commitment to the survival of an independent South Vietnam grew dramatically during the administration of John F. Kennedy, the president supported the idea of making the Special Forces a major instrument in a counterinsurgency plan to help the Saigon government meet the threat of armed subversion by the Vietcong. In September 1961 the army activated the Fifth Special Forces Group (Airborne) at Fort Bragg. Small numbers of Green Berets had already been training South Vietnamese Special Forces and ARVN Ranger companies in reconnaissance techniques and other skills, and Kennedy now sent 400 additional Green Berets to Vietnam in the first phase of what became an escalating military advisory mission.

One of the key tasks given to the Special Forces was to help the Saigon government block infiltration, fight the insurgents, and regain its authority in the Central Highlands. To accomplish this mission, the Special Forces advisers organized the mountain people, mostly non-Vietnamese ethnic minorities whom the former French colonial governors had collectively labeled Montagnards, into units that became known as the Civilian Irregular Defense Group (CIDG). Small teams of eight to fourteen Green Berets worked with RVN Special Forces counterparts to advise the CIDG in construction of fortified camps from which they could provide village security and conduct patrols to disrupt Vietcong activity in their area of operations. The quality and loyalty of the CIDG and of the Green Berets' South Vietnamese counterparts varied greatly. There was frequent ethnic tension between the Montagnards and the Vietnamese soldiers. In addition to the CIDG program, Special Forces personnel also became engaged in civic action projects (such as digging wells and building schools in the villages), long-range reconnaissance training of U.S. forces, and intelligence gathering and other covert operations along the Cambodian and Laotian borders.

Before FitzGibbon arrived in Vietnam in 1968, the role of the U.S. military in South Vietnam had changed significantly from that of the early 1960s, when the Special Forces advisers first arrived in significant numbers. The escalation of the number of American ground combat forces in South Vietnam that began in 1965 and surpassed the half million mark in early 1968 meant that the military conduct of the war against the Vietcong and NVA had come to be characterized by the use of large-unit sweeps to find the enemy and high technology weaponry to destroy enemy forces. Village security and pacification—that is, trying to build support among the people for the Saigon government—had been overshadowed by these conventional warfare tactics, which often included air and artillery bombardment that created civilian casualties. General William C. Westmoreland, who had overall command of American ground operations in South Vietnam, had declared in late 1967 that this attrition strategy of inflicting heavy losses on the communist forces was weakening the enemy and bringing the end of the war into view. The ability of the Vietcong to launch the Tet Offensive throughout the South (even considering that the offensive stalled) had challenged this assertion of military progress based on attrition and placed renewed emphasis on pacification as a better approach. In July 1968 General Creighton Abrams succeeded Westmoreland as commander in Vietnam, and he began to shift U.S. strategy from attrition to pacification, small-unit operations, and Vietnamization (that is, greater operational responsibility for South Vietnamese forces). This form of warfare much better suited the training and mission of the Special Forces.

In his letters home, FitzGibbon commented from time to time on the way the war was being fought. In contrast to the highly censored mail of World War II, letters sent from soldiers in Vietnam were often quite revealing and are an excellent historical source.

**President Lyndon B. Johnson with General William C. Westmoreland
reviewing troops at Cam Ranh Bay in 1966.**
Time Life Pictures/Getty Images

FitzGibbon was an astute observer, and his doubts about the way the war was being fought were similar to debates over tactics and strategy that went on at higher command levels and that have continued to preoccupy the work of military historians since the war. In some ways his critical comments are the classic refrain of the combat soldier: "This is a heck of a way to run a war." In many ways, however, the insights he committed to paper in his bunker in his A camp were accurate assessments of at least some of the reasons the United States failed to accomplish its overall objective of preserving a separate and independent Republic of Vietnam. He noted disapprovingly, for example, how the large-unit combat operations that he observed netted few North Vietnamese killed or captured. One of the big problems, in his view, was the extremely complex and ambiguous chain of command both within the U.S. military organization in South Vietnam and between the ARVN and American commanders. FitzGibbon got along fairly well with Lieutenant Lang, his ARVN counterpart, but he found that, in general, a lack of trust hampered American and South Vietnamese operational coordination. During much of his time at Ha Tay, he shared a tactical area of operations with the U.S. Army's 173rd Airborne Brigade, and he was especially critical of the brigade commander's lack of understanding of the CIDG. His letters speak directly to historical debates that continue today on attrition versus pacification, large-unit versus small-unit operations, the training and doctrine of the U.S. Army in Vietnam, and the relationship between Americans in South Vietnam and their South Vietnamese allies.

After about three months in Vietnam, FitzGibbon had come to believe that the war would not turn out well for the United States. Visiting the U.S. military hospital in Pleiku, he was shocked to see the physical price that American soldiers were paying, when, from what he had seen in tactical operations, the United States was not breaking up the Vietcong's organizational infrastructure and North Vietnamese infiltration into South Vietnam. The Vietcong would continue to survive politically, in his estimation, and eventually force the United States out. The point would come, in other words, when the United States would reach a limit of what price it was willing to pay to sustain a South Vietnamese regime of questionable integrity. Despite this pragmatic and prescient assessment, FitzGibbon never wavered in his belief that the principles behind American military intervention in Vietnam were appropriate. After seeing the John Wayne movie, *The Green Berets*, which was released in 1968, he declared that he liked it because he believed in the story it depicted of protecting the lives and freedom of Vietnamese threatened by communist dictatorship. He did, however, find the film's portrayal of combat to be "laughable."

In October the Fifth Special Forces Group transferred FitzGibbon to command of the A-team camp at Duc Lap, located southwest of Ban Me Thuot and right on the border with Cambodia. The camp was only a few miles from a major NVA base area inside Cambodia, had been temporarily overrun in August by an enemy assault, and remained a vulnerable and dangerous location. This troubled camp had a host of organizational and equipment problems, and FitzGibbon's selection for this post revealed the confidence his commanders had in him. By the end of the year, he was stationed at the group headquarters in Nha Trang in a key staff position that included briefing General Abrams and other top American military brass. He extended his tour of duty in Vietnam beyond the one year that was standard procedure and remained in the rear-echelon position until he prepared to leave the army in the fall of 1969 to begin studies at Harvard Law School.

A secondary theme in these letters beyond the excellent reporting they provide on military conduct of the war is how soldiers in Vietnam were able to remain closely connected to life back in "the world," as the GIs often referred to the United States. Even while he was stationed at remote Special Forces camps in the coastal lowlands and Central Highlands of II Corps, FitzGibbon prepared for the law school admissions test, applied to several law schools, followed closely the political campaigns at home, and in other ways remained engaged in life in the United States. Although historians sometimes make distinctions between the war in Vietnam and the war at home—that is, the domestic controversy spawned by the war—American soldiers in the combat and support areas were well aware of domestic life and issues in the United States. During the 1968–69 period in which FitzGibbon served in Vietnam, the level of public criticism of the war and outright opposition to it increased notably, and it was a trend that was on his mind as his tour of duty drew to a close in the summer of 1969.

As FitzGibbon looked back, he continued to believe that the war was worthwhile, but he made no assertions that it was winnable for the United States in a military sense. He acknowledged that the political regime in South Vietnam suffered from corruption and was not a model of democracy, but he maintained that it was a better system than communist dictatorship. On the subject of the way the war was being conducted, his opinions reflected a view of many in the military that the Johnson administration's original strategy of gradual escalation had not worked. The better approach, he believed, needed to be either an all-out application of American military might or a genuine pacification strategy that placed primary responsibility for success on the RVN government itself with U.S. advisers such as the Special Forces. By 1969 U.S. policy in Vietnam was moving in the latter direction

**American Secretary of State Henry Kissinger and Vietnamese politician Le Duc Tho
sign the Paris peace accords that ended the Vietnam War. Both men were
awarded the Nobel Peace Prize but Le Duc Tho refused to accept it.**
Getty Images

under the heading of Vietnamization. As a realist, however, he departed from Vietnam expressing doubts that the country was better off than when he arrived, and his hope was only that the war would not drag on much longer.

FitzGibbon's letters reveal that sometimes individual courage and common sense are not enough. His courage, which he attributed to training and excitement more than bravery, came from his willingness to fight for the principles of justice for which he believed the United States stood. His commonsense assessments of the situation as he saw it derived from critical thinking skills that would eventually make him a successful attorney. Like many other American soldiers, FitzGibbon did what he was supposed to do in Vietnam and did it well. American policies in Vietnam did not always meet the same standard.

David L. Anderson is dean of the College of Undergraduate Programs at California State University, Monterey Bay. He is the former dean of the College of Arts and Sciences at the University of Indianapolis, where he taught history for twenty-three years. His books include The Human Tradition in America since 1945 *(2003);* The Columbia Guide to the Vietnam War *(2002);* The Human Tradition in the Vietnam Era *(2000);* Facing My Lai: Moving Beyond the Massacre *(1998);* Trapped by Success: The Eisenhower Administration and the Vietnam War *(1991) (winner of the Robert H. Ferrell Book Prize from the Society for Historians of American Foreign Relations); and* Imperialism and Idealism: American Diplomats in China *(1985). He has served on the editorial board of* Diplomatic History *and as president of the Society for Historians of American Foreign Relations. He was in the U.S. Army from 1968 to 1970 and served in the Vietnam War as a sergeant in the Signal Corps.*

Lenore and Joseph FitzGibbon, the author's parents.
Daniel H. FitzGibbon

PREFACE

This book is drawn from the letters I wrote home to my parents, Joseph and Lenore FitzGibbon, in Columbus, Indiana, while I was serving in Vietnam during 1968 and 1969. My original intention was to compile what would amount to a journal or diary describing virtually everything of significance I did, saw, or felt. As you will see, and as with many New Year's resolutions, my intention and initial efforts were far superior to my ultimate results. My early letters were voluminous, but after the novelty of Vietnam service wore off and my workload expanded, they became fewer and further between, to the point my parents even asked the American Red Cross to check whether I still existed. (Seriously!)

My mother kept the letters, such as they were, and gave them to me sometime in the early 1980s. In 1988 I decided to have the letters typed and copies made for my children so that they would know "what Daddy did in the war." At that time I filled in many of the gaps by inserting a number of other incidents, experiences, observations, and emotions, all of which were as authentic as I could make them after twenty years, to provide as complete a record as I could for my children.

These letters, then, are not verbatim transcripts of the originals. Aside from the additions noted above, I have made other changes to provide background, clarify military unit designations and jargon, and generally make it easier for the nonveteran to follow. In addition, I altered or deleted some statements that I thought, in retrospect, were unfair or at least uncharitable to certain individuals and removed several names. I also struck several portions to avoid intruding unnecessarily on private or personal matters. These letters, after all, were originally written for my parents' private consumption and not for publication.

Even as edited, the letters are sometimes disjointed and unbalanced. Most of them were written in stages over several days or weeks as I found time to enter my thoughts, so there are abrupt changes in subject matter and style, a few inconsistent comments, and some repetition of topics. My entries often reflected my moods and emotions at the time I made them, as well as my own self-absorption with my narrow mission and responsibilities, so they were not very fair or objective. Lacking other outlets, I used the letters to vent my frustrations and worries, usually without bothering to note the offsetting positive sides of events and people.

I should note that many statements in my letters were based solely or largely on third-party reports, gossip, or speculation, even though they are written as if they were gospel. The rumor mill in a wartime army takes on a life and stature far out of proportion to its evidentiary merit. I cannot vouch, especially after all these years, for the accuracy of any reported incident, characteristic, or circumstance I did not personally participate in or witness.

In reading these letters, you will find that the author often appears to be unduly full of himself and impressed with his own wisdom, courage, and competence. Knowing him as I do, I suspect he was every bit as insecure and afraid as anyone would be in his situation. I am sure that his bravado and self-importance reveal an effort to persuade himself that he measured up to his own hopes and expectations, and to make his parents, his only intended audience, proud of him. I hope that the reader will be more forgiving of his flaws than I am.

I would like to acknowledge and thank the Indiana Historical Society, and specifically Roy Shoemaker, Ray Boomhower, Tom

Mason, and Sal Cilella, who read the letters and somehow considered them worthy of publication by that illustrious institution; Professor David Anderson, for his gracious and informative foreword; my Vietnam War comrades, and especially my Special Forces team members, who served their country faithfully, honorably, and courageously in an unusually difficult and controversial conflict; my parents, for all that they did for me; my children, Kathy and Tom, who inspired me to assemble and edit these letters in 1988 and will always be my greatest pride and joy; and my wife, Joan, for her patience, support, and devotion not only during the preparation of this edition but on all matters throughout more than thirty years of marriage.

Daniel FitzGibbon
Indianapolis, Indiana
Spring 2004

INTRODUCTION

Three decades after the last American ground units withdrew from South Vietnam and the subsequent conquest of that country by North Vietnam, the war remains a highly contentious and emotional subject for many Americans who lived through the era. While most Americans presumably agree that the outcome was disastrous, they continue to be deeply divided over the merits and scope of our involvement, the strategies we employed, and the general conduct of the war. I will not attempt to explore, let alone resolve, these issues in this introduction. I do, however, believe an abbreviated account of the background and rationale of intervention by the United States, based on my understanding then and now, would provide useful context.

At the conclusion of the French Indochina War in 1954, France gave up its colonial claims to Vietnam and the rest of Indochina and agreed with the insurgent Viet Minh (led by the communist Ho Chi Minh but comprised of many noncommunist nationalist forces) to a partition of the country into communist North Vietnam and noncommunist South Vietnam. A unification referendum was to be held two years later, but South Vietnam refused to go along since it was not a party to the 1954 agreement and, pragmatically, recognized that North Vietnam (with its larger population and tightly controlled electorate) would dictate the outcome. Beginning in the late 1950s, North Vietnam activated communist cadres in the South (the Vietcong or VC) and infiltrated other troops, as well as arms and supplies provided by the Soviet Union, into the South in an effort to take the country by force. The United States saw this insurgency as yet another in a series of attempts by communist factions dating from 1945 (starting with eastern Europe and continuing with China, the Philippines, Korea, Malaya, Cuba, and other countries) to seize power militarily. The Soviet Union declared it would support "wars of national liberation," and North Vietnam's actions appeared to fit that mold. Fearing the continued spread of an aggressive, totalitarian, and often brutal communist system, the United States decided Vietnam was the place to draw the line.

America was concerned that its actions might trigger armed involvement by the Soviet Union or China and lead to a wider war. It therefore pursued intervention through incremental escalations of force and manpower and restricted both the weaponry and the targets available to its military command. Initially sending only American military advisers (including Army Special Forces units) with limited air support, the United States found it necessary to begin inserting conventional American army and marine ground forces in March 1965, when communist troops appeared to be on the verge of success. By the time I arrived in early 1968, more than 500,000 Americans were already in-country. The United States (and certain other foreign allies, such as South Korea) had assumed responsibility for the heaviest combat roles, conducting large operations along NVA infiltration routes and in NVA/VC base areas. Meanwhile, the South Vietnamese Army (ARVN) took over local security functions for the major populated areas. To a great extent, this had become an American war.

The 1968 Tet Offensive, which the VC initiated in violation of an agreed cease-fire, brought them military disaster but political success. The war was perceived by many in the United States as a stalemate, a quagmire consuming endless lives and resources on both sides, with no positive end in sight.

Tet thus marked the beginning of the end for Lyndon B. Johnson's presidency and, eventually, American involvement in Vietnam. In June 1969 the United States began to "Vietnamize" the war, turning combat responsibility back to ARVN forces and pulling out major American ground units over a three-year period. In early 1973 the Paris peace accords were signed, the United States withdrew all remaining troops, and prisoners of war were repatriated. Two years later, North Vietnam launched a major invasion of South Vietnam in violation of the peace accords while the United States stood passively by, leading to the demise of the South Vietnam government in April 1975. The Vietnam War was over, and the country was reunified under a communist government.

As noted previously, Army Special Forces soldiers were among the American military advisers sent to South Vietnam during the early stages of the war. Despite the presence of large regular American combat units starting in 1965, there was still a major role to be played by Special Forces personnel while I was there. The primary Special Forces unit in Vietnam during my tenure was the Fifth Special Forces Group.

By way of background, the U.S. Army Special Forces are primarily designed for unconventional, or guerrilla, warfare, by recruiting, organizing, training, and equipping local partisan forces in countries controlled by the enemy, then leading or advising these forces in combat and related operations against enemy troops and facilities. In South Vietnam, our role was essentially reversed; the VC conducted guerrilla warfare against the established government and its armed forces, so we conducted counterinsurgency operations. We employed our locally recruited forces to seek out and engage the VC, using a combination of intelligence activities, small patrols, ambushes, and large unit sweeps. We also conducted combat operations, sometimes in coordination with regular American combat forces and air/artillery support, against major NVA units based in or passing through our assigned areas. In addition, we carried out the important added functions of promoting civil government, providing medical care and hygiene assistance to local civilians, organizing construction projects, and conducting psychological operations.

The basic Special Forces unit was (and is) the A team, which in Vietnam consisted of three officers (a commanding officer, an executive officer, and a civil affairs/psychological operations officer) and ten experienced noncommissioned officers (NCOs). The A team's NCOs were highly trained (and cross-trained) in specialties such as heavy and light weapons, engineering and demolitions, intelligence, communications, and medicine. Each A team operated from a base camp in a remote part of the countryside and was responsible for an area of operations typically covering several hundred square miles. The American A team advised a Vietnamese Special Forces counterpart A team that technically commanded the locally recruited CIDG forces. The CIDG troops, which numbered several hundred in each camp, were paramilitary units not subject to military law and discipline.

The next larger Special Forces unit, controlling several A teams, was called a B team, and overseeing several B teams was, naturally, a C team (sometimes called a company). South Vietnam was divided militarily into four Corps areas, and there was a separate Special Forces C team for each Corps area. The four C teams and some other units reported to the Fifth Special Forces Group in Nha Trang.

By early 1968 there were around eighty Special Forces A teams and camps spread throughout the country, many alongside major NVA infiltration routes by the Laotian and Cambodian borders. Others were in provinces suffering especially heavy concentra-

The author with his mother, Lenore, at the John F. Kennedy Special Warfare Center, Fort Bragg, North Carolina. FitzGibbon is holding his honor graduate award for finishing first out of 177 officers in the Special Forces Officers Course, September 1967.
Daniel H. FitzGibbon

tions of VC and NVA units. Our general strategy was to create an effective CIDG fighting force and secure environment in each of these critical locations and, once the area was relatively pacified, convert the CIDG into a regional militia under the control of district and provincial officials or into a regular ARVN unit. The American and Vietnamese Special Forces teams would then move on to a new and more challenging location and repeat the process with other CIDG troops recruited from the local populace.

When I arrived in Vietnam, I was twenty-five years old, having graduated from West Point and the Army's Airborne, Ranger, and Special Forces schools. I had also been given intensive instruction in demolitions and the Vietnamese language. In addition, I had served almost three years in West Berlin, where I participated in both training operations and occasionally tense Cold War situations, before volunteering for Vietnam. I felt reasonably well prepared for that unnatural state of affairs known as combat and approached my new assignment with enthusiasm and belief in our cause. While I had already decided to resign from the army and become a lawyer, I wanted first to do my part in the war as a combat infantry officer.

In my first eight months in Vietnam, from February through October 1968, I commanded a Special Forces A team based at a camp called Ha Tay. This camp was a small outpost surrounded by rice paddies, a few villages, and many steep, forested mountains near the central coast of South Vietnam, in an area populated primarily by ethnic Vietnamese (as opposed to various ethnic minorities). Our CIDG forces at Ha Tay were converted into regional militia in March 1969, some five months after I left the camp. After Ha Tay, I took charge of another A team for a couple of months at Duc Lap in the Central Highlands of South Vietnam near the Cambodian border, an area of rolling hills, thick

6

vegetation, and rubber plantations. Duc Lap was part of a region occupied almost exclusively by various nomadic ethnic hill tribes that the French collectively called Montagnards. I left Duc Lap in December 1968 to become a staff officer in the S-3 (operations and training) section of Fifth Special Forces Group headquarters in Nha Trang. The Duc Lap camp continued under Special Forces control after my departure until the end of 1970, when its CIDG force became an ARVN Ranger battalion. My extended Vietnam tour of duty ended in late August 1969, when I returned to the United States, resigned my commission, and entered law school.

In February 1971, as part of Vietnamization, the Fifth Special Forces Group pulled out of South Vietnam, marking the end of a nine-year period of American Special Forces involvement in that country. Four years later, the war was over.

10 Feb. 1968

Dear Folks:

Just a brief note to let you know I arrived OK and am still safe and sound in Nha Trang. Haven't moved to my final camp yet because of the distractions created by the Tet offensive and a major attack on the Special Forces camp at Lang Vei. Had I known the Vietcong (VC) and North Vietnamese Army (NVA) were going to react so negatively to my arrival, I might have stayed home!

I flew out of McChord Air Force Base (Ft. Lewis, Washington) at 10:30 a.m. local time (1:30 p.m. your time) on 5 Feb. After a 10½ hour flight (on a Northwest Orient jet) we landed in Tokyo but sat in the plane for 1½ hours before taking off again. They wouldn't let us get off—apparently, the nine sailors who took a similar occasion to desert at Yokohama taught them a lesson. We flew on 5½ hours more and landed at Cam Ranh Bay 7:00 a.m. your time 6 Feb. or 8:00 p.m. Vietnam time 6 Feb., so we're 13 hours ahead of you (crossed international date line, gained a day and started losing time).

You know how one's view of a place is shaped by its portrayal in the media. Every time there's an article or TV piece on Vietnam the place seems to be on fire or under mortar attack, so I half expected incoming artillery shells to be exploding all around my plane when we flew in. Instead it was very quiet and dark, without even the usual lights and noises one expects at an airport and surrounding city.

I stayed at Cam Ranh for 1½ days waiting for my orders to be confirmed for the Fifth Special Forces Group (Airborne). As you know, even though I'm Special Forces qualified, I've been assigned to U.S. Army Vietnam (USARV) since last May and my assignment to the Fifth Special Forces Group was not final until I arrived in-country, but the orders eventually came through OK. Cam Ranh is a massive logistics base and port on the South China Sea, the eastern coast of Vietnam. I saw only the Army replacement compound, and I can imagine how vast it must be when you throw in the Navy, Air Force, and rest of the Army setup. Weather is hot—75 degrees at night with pleasant sea breeze, 95 degrees during day with no breeze. Beautiful white sand and blue water. Cam Ranh is so secure you wouldn't know a war's going on except for armed sentries, bunkers, and periodic flares at night. It serves as an in-country rest and recuperation (R & R) area with water skiing and boating going on, all of which is sort of unreal when you think about it. I slept on a bunk in a wooden building—latrine and shower in separate building 50 meters away. Nice mess hall—standard American food and plenty of it. I got my currency converted to Military Payment Currency (MPC's—scrip), for use in all American facilities in lieu of dollars; the local currency is piastres but I won't need that until later. I boxed up my dress green uniform, shirt, and tie and mailed them home to you—you should get them about the time you receive this letter. There was an officer's club with plenty of cokes and booze. No real sense of urgency among administrative personnel here—they're more casual by far then we were in my last assignment in West Berlin. Thurs. a.m., I caught a chopper up the coast to Nha Trang—a beautiful ride along the bay and beach over to the Special Forces compound, HQ of the Fifth Special Forces Group.

The compound here in Nha Trang is less secure than Cam Ranh, hence a greater sense of urgency. During the recent Tet attacks in the city several personnel from here got killed jumping into jeeps and riding through town as if this were some rah-rah game rather than a war. The compound here is surrounded by hills—all VC controlled. One of the hills is held by a VC rocket battalion—I sit out by HQ each evening with a beer in my hand and watch our Air Force drop bombs on it. The whole spectacle is so remote and impersonal it seems I'm watching a demonstration or drive-in movie. The hill is about 3 miles away—within easy range of our compound. Each night Charlie (VC) lobs a few mortar rounds into the compound but achieves few results. Operations and Intelligence here expect a full-scale attack anytime, but I suspect they're overplaying the real danger (I like to make fun of rear-echelon HQ types as if I were a hard-bitten frontline infantryman, even though I'm yet to work my way to the front lines myself!). Between the hills and this compound is a huge rice paddy—very flat so that any VC attack across it would be suicide. If they come they'll probably infiltrate around the paddy and storm in from the sides, while firing rockets and mortars from the far hills. Meanwhile, you don't know whether, or when, anything's going to happen, and it all seems unreal.

When I arrived I was interviewed by the adjutant (head of Personnel and Administration) and asked my choice of assignment. I chose II Corps area, which for the Fifth Special Forces Group means Company B. The Republic of Vietnam (RVN) runs I, II, III, & IV Corps areas, north to south. II Corps is the largest, with HQ at Pleiku. Most of my friends from Forts Bragg (North Carolina) and Bliss (Texas), where I had my Special Forces and Vietnamese language training, are in II Corps, not that they would be serving with me. Since my arrival I have been processing records and getting briefings and orientations and not really doing a whole lot. Nels Marin, a fellow Special Forces captain and close friend from Berlin, is stationed here as one of the three assistant adjutants. Bob Mack, another Berlin friend, is the A team commanding officer (CO) at Dong Xoai. I won't know where I'm going until I get to Pleiku (pronounced play-coo), but was notified by phone that they would like to make me adjutant there because I did some of that work in Berlin. I'd much rather get an A team and camp, since I volunteered to come here to be in combat rather than a staff position and I'd hate to become one of those rear-echelon types I've already been making fun of. I guess I'll have to fight that one out when I get to Pleiku.

The problem with my departure from here is getting a flight to Pleiku. The recent troubles have limited flights to combat essentials, but I hope things let up enough for me to fly out tomorrow (Sunday). If I do get an A camp, I probably won't arrive there for another 3–4 days at least.

The facilities here at Nha Trang are very nice—plush officers' club, running hot-cold water, movie theater, and real commodes. I can't believe how nice it is. The transient billets are pretty bad, however, with close rows of double bunk beds and suitcases and carbines all over. I was issued an M-2 carbine, but hope to exchange it later for an M-16 or CAR-15 rifle. I may scrounge a pistol if I can.

By the way, I picked up an ear infection before leaving Washington—apparently from that cold I had. It still bothers me, but a variety of ear drops, pills, penicillin, etc. is apparently working out OK. At least it gave me something else to think about when I was flying into Vietnam!

Well, that's it for now. I'll try to write a little bit each night when I get settled and put it all together for mailing about once a week or two. It should serve as sort of a diary. By the way, my return address is not final yet, but any letters you send to Company B, etc., will eventually reach me.

Love,
Dan

24 Feb. 1968

Dear Folks:

I haven't received a letter from you yet but assume nothing has caught up with me at my new address. I hope my last letter, check, and package with uniform made it OK. My new address is DET A-227, Fifth SFG(A), APO SF 96234.

This letter is going to be pretty disorganized, since I'm doing a little at a time and bouncing to and from various topics as I go from one writing opportunity to the next.

To bring you up to date on my resettlement process, I finally departed Nha Trang for Pleiku on Sunday, 11 Feb. 1968. The night before, however, Fifth Special Forces Group HQ was sure of a VC attack and called an alert for 0400 Sunday morning (the VC usually hit at about midnight to allow plenty of time before daylight—nevertheless, alert was at 0400). Furthermore, the alert signal is one siren blast—all clear is a second siren blast. They blew two sirens about 5 minutes apart, so I assumed the all clear was on. Nevertheless, I walked outside (unarmed) to observe what was happening since I could still see U.S. Air Force (USAF) flare ships dropping illumination and artillery pounding the hill where rockets are suspected. All at once a belligerent individual in steel pot, etc., approached, demanding to know where my weapon was. I assumed he was a sergeant, so I was embarrassed for him when he would find out I was a captain. He turned out to be a major, so I was embarrassed for myself instead. He claimed the second siren was blown to "confirm" the first, notwithstanding their own alert procedure. So I shrugged my shoulders, stumbled off for my rifle, and headed for a concrete bunker inhabited by an over-ranked squad of captains, majors, and lieutenant colonels. It seems the officers all live on one side of the compound and run to the same row of bunkers where they can least influence the action. Anyway, after 30 minutes of waiting, my friend the major returned, had all inside the bunker get out and go to bed and all outside go in and sit, and so I wandered off to bed still confused. Maybe I'll figure all this out (and, even worse, start behaving the same way) once I've been here a few months.

That morning it rained heavily, with fog, but I managed to get on a flight of six choppers headed for Pleiku. We moved up the coast about 30 minutes until the fog worsened and had to return. I managed to scrounge an Air Force C-123 heading to Pleiku shortly thereafter, so I transferred three bags and one carbine in the rain and took the one hour flight to Pleiku.

I was met at Pleiku by Jerry Turcotte—a good friend from Forts Bragg and Bliss who is operations officer for Company B, the control headquarters for Special Forces operations in II Corps. Jerry was concerned about the danger of mortar/ground attacks, although I'm told no Americans had been killed from VC attacks at the Pleiku base since Gulf of Tonkin days four years ago, and the Pleiku/Camp Holloway area houses not only Special Forces but a logistics command base, Fourth Infantry Division headquarters, a field hospital, and a large USAF base, and is well protected terrain-wise. Seems Pleiku city was hit during Tet and several of the Special Forces staff all participated in cleaning-up operations in the city. Anyway, I found out that I was not wanted for adjutant, but rather for assistant operations officer for about a month, then intelligence officer, for Company B. That might sound interesting, but I'd already figured out that the higher HQ Special Forces units have very little direct effect on the real war and that the intelligence officer would do little more than relay information up and down. Eager to do something more meaningful with my time over here and apply my military skills and experiences, I fought, wept, scratched, clawed, and otherwise made myself obnoxious pushing for an A team. I had planned to report to the Colonel needing a shave, booze on my breath, and my fly open to impress him with my unworthiness and subsequent undesirability for a staff job, but was fortunately warned in time that such appearance would fit in with the remainder of the staff officers and achieve the opposite effect! Anyway, I succeeded in conquering the obstacles and was assigned to B-22, the easternmost of the three subordinate control HQ in II Corps, based at Qui Nhon (pronounced Kwee Nyon) on the coast above Nha Trang and Tuy Hoa, about due east of Pleiku.

When I arrived at Pleiku, incidentally, the sun was shining and the weather somewhat cooler (with the higher elevation of the Central Highlands). There is a swimming pool by the Officers' Club on the C team compound, and Sunday evening I went to the Seventy-first Hospital Officers Club to a steak barbecue. How bad is that? I also wore a civilian shirt and slacks. There were about 30 nurses there and none of them suffered from inattention. Anyway, the whole scene seemed unreal and I felt a little out of place to be in a war and still live well and securely. Contrary to most Americans' ideas and impressions, Vietnam is not a series of incoming mortar rounds and terrorist grenades, but actually a generally quiet area, particularly in places like Pleiku. I should be more generous to these HQ people, however, since they at least are here in VN trying to do something to help.

I had to stay at Pleiku from Sunday through Thursday (11th to 15th), partly for orientations by each staff section and partly to await transportation to Qui Nhon. It seemed no helicopters or USAF planes were heading that way, so I almost caught a C-123 for Cam Ranh Bay (regressing on my journey, it would seem) for a shuttle run north to Qui Nhon. Instead, on Thursday I called my

B team HQ at Qui Nhon to request some assistance. Fortunately, they had a chopper going to Pleiku that afternoon taking the operations officer to a briefing that I could catch for the return trip.

I arrived at Qui Nhon on Thursday evening, met the staff and my immediate commander, Lt. Col. Longfellow, the B team leader, a friendly easy-going guy. Qui Nhon is on the east coast, as I said, and also houses an ARVN [Army of Republic of South Vietnam] HQ, a MACV [Military Assistance Command, Vietnam—advisers to ARVN units and suppliers] HQ and a naval port squadron where some supplies are landed. The B team is located in an old villa complex, right on the sea with beautiful white sand all around. I understand they used to charcoal-broil steaks on the sand and all other such stuff (they have a boat), but things were not that nice at the time I arrived. The Tet offensive and sporadic incidents related thereto were still in progress, so most of the staff were committed to that action. Since only a few elements of the Korean (ROK) First Division were available to handle things in the Qui Nhon area, Lt. Col. Longfellow had to pull companies up from his A camps and use them in the operation, under his personal control. About 30 of the native company members were killed, as were the U.S. B team intelligence officer and assistant operations officer the day before I arrived.

I was told I was being sent to the Ha Tay (pronounced as it looks) Special Forces camp to be A team leader there; each time this was mentioned I detected knowing exchanges of smirks, a few shrugs of "another sheep for the slaughter," some pats of sympathy, and a general desire for disassociation in case what I was about to get was contagious. People looked around to see who was watching and made sure the coast was clear while talking with me. For some reason, I developed some misgivings about the assignment, but of course plunged ahead with boundless optimism!

Anyway, Lt. Col. Longfellow decided to let me first see some other camps in his sector, so sent me south to Dong Tre on Friday morning to get an idea of their layout. The A team leader there attended the Special Forces course in my class at Fort Bragg but did not go to language school with me. I arrived there not long after a mortar round accidentally injured several children and killed some cows. The camp has three 81 mm mortars, and each one must be registered (that is, sighted by position and angle) on distinct terrain features in the area. Registration provides confirmed data to place on the mortar sight in the event these terrain features are used by the VC for their own rocket/mortar emplacements, so we can hit them back immediately without going through the usual estimation and trial and error process. It also provides a known point from which other locations of VC strength can be referred and fired on with minimal calculations required. The registration point (RP) in question was located in a Free Fire Zone—an area where Vietnamese officials had declared no civilians could live or work and where all persons seen were presumed to be VC and could be taken under fire. The nearby villagers were also told that the hill in question would be bombarded that day, but somehow four kids and about 35 cattle were right there and the round landed in the middle. Fortunately the kids were only wounded and were evacuated OK, and of course we ended up paying the villagers for their dead and wounded cattle (which they promptly butchered and ate). It was definitely a shame and probably unavoidable but it seemed to me that the mortar could have been fired after 1800 (6:00 p.m.) when no people would be in the fields and while enough daylight remained to observe adequately, and that the mortar observer calling in the firing directions and corrections could have been positioned close enough to the target to insure the coast was clear. Too many people at the camp shrugged the incident off as unavoidable, but it seemed to me that in spite of our good intentions and rapid reimbursement, these incidents drive a wedge between the villagers and our cause and prompt the victims of such actions to sympathize with the VC. A mortar round is still a mortar round, regardless of the good intentions of those firing it. Maybe I'll harden after I've been here awhile.

After two days there, I left Dong Tre on Sunday morning, flew to Cung Son for about a one hour stopover where I met Leo Mercier, the A team leader, who was also in my Special Forces class. Saw his layout and returned to Qui Nhon, got an intelligence briefing and took off in an O-1 light observation plane with Ben Glawe, a USAF FAC (Forward Air Controller), for a spin through my new Tactical Area of Responsibility (TAOR) and into my new A camp, Ha Tay. Ben has flown everything from these light planes to jet fighters to bombers, and enjoys flying upside down, doing barrel rolls, diving, and generally trying to make me throw up which is not too difficult; we've now been up together (Ben, I, and my breakfast) a couple of times already. Ha Tay is about 50 miles NW of Qui Nhon, about 15 miles inland, about 10 miles south of Bong Son and in a heavy mountainous area with thick vegetation. The mountains here are very steep, with comparatively bare peaks.

Detachments are numbered by size/type (A is smallest, B is control HQ for several As, C is control HQ for several Bs) and location. My A team is in II Corps area, is controlled by the second of three (formerly four) B teams in this C team or Corps area, and is the seventh (at one time—now there are three) A team in that B team sector. My detachment number is thus A-227. Each A team is authorized 13 men: a Captain commanding officer (me), a First Lieutenant (1LT) Executive Officer (XO), a 1LT Civil

Affairs/Psychological Operations (CA/PO) officer, and ten NCOs from buck sergeant to master sergeant who are highly trained specialists (but cross-trained) in the areas of Operations/Intelligence, Weapons, Communications, Demolitions/Engineering, and Medicine/Hygiene.

Ha Tay, as I stated, is just west of the rice basin and in a heavy mountainous area, with streams in the claw-shaped valleys, thick and tall elephant grass along the streams, rice paddies with standing water in the flat areas, and thick foliage all around. My "Tactical Area of Operational Responsibility," or TAOR, covers about 400 square km of area (about 150 sq. miles). Ground elevation is about 100 feet. The camp is the only Special Forces A camp in Binh Dinh Province, one of about 20 in II Corps and about 80 in the entire country. It is only about eight months old, having been transferred about 15 km south from Bong Son when the Army's First Cavalry Division moved its HQ up there. It is therefore only partially completed, and much work remains. It has a 1,600 foot runway (can take up to a C-7A Caribou fixed-wing airplane) for resupply runs, and is basically graded dirt covered with peneprime, a tar-like oil. I have no idea how long the U.S. Special Forces team will remain here, but the goal is to finish the place in about nine more months, turn it over to the Vietnamese Special Forces team or an ARVN unit, and relocate into a hotter area (that is, NVA/VC controlled) near Cambodia or Laos. Several A camps in this area have already been transferred, but much work remains before this one can. I just hope Charlie (VC) cooperates and doesn't try to overrun us in the process.

The camp itself is located on the forward edge and top of the smaller of two adjoining hills, and is ⅔ encircled by larger hills and vegetation-covered draws (shallow gullies) less than 300 meters away. The other ⅓, where the runway is, is flat with rice paddies,

**The Ha Tay Special Forces Camp. The photograph was taken by FitzGibbon
from an airplane from the south of the camp, looking north.
The Kim Son River is in the background.**
Daniel H. FitzGibbon

and has a river and dirt road (shown on the map as "Highway" 506, which is a stretch) running along the valley east/southeast of camp. Highway 506 runs into Highway 1 about 10 miles to the southeast (Highway 1 is the famous *Rue Sans Joie*—Street Without Joy—from French Indochina days). On the other side of the runway by the rice paddies is an American artillery battery (with two 175 mm guns and two 8 inch howitzers), two Dusters (track-mounted twin 40 mm rocket launchers that spew grenades like machine gun bullets), and presently an infantry platoon with two 4.2 inch mortars for security. The cracks of the 8s and double cracks ("whomp-whomp") of the 175s day and night are incredibly loud and the concussions rattle my bunkers, especially when the firing is southward over my camp, but since many of their missions are against targets I select based on intelligence reports from my agents I'm in no position to complain to the neighbors.

On the three hills around the camp I have outposts of 10–15 native troops each, who rotate every few days. Surrounding the camp itself are rows of fences/concertina (circular accordion-like barbed wire), with one row of Claymore mines (which send lead fragments in a wide forward arc when detonated electronically) around part of the perimeter. I have an inner perimeter (separated by concertina) in which my team living quarters, tactical operations center (TOC), two 106 mm recoilless rifles, three 81 mm mortars, three 50 cal. machine guns, one 4.2 inch mortar, and various other small arms and 60 mm mortars are located. There are four companies on the outer perimeter, living in bunkers, and two combat reconnaissance (recon) platoons. Each company has 133 men authorized, but only about 100 actually assigned. The troops are Vietnamese Civilian Irregular Defense Group (CIDG) troops—basically civilians who have been recruited voluntarily and to whom no military code nor disciplinary jurisdiction applies. We train them ourselves, outfit them and take them on operations. I'm told they have a tendency to "terminate their enlistment" when things get tough, and we can't stop them. Sometimes they walk off with uniform, weapons, and equipment, reportedly for eventual sale or gift to Charlie. Their light armament, poor discipline, and limited training make them generally a poor match for the NVA troops unless we catch the NVA at a time when we outnumber them or have access to air or artillery support (which is rare out in the boonies). One of the companies consists of Montagnards (four different mountain tribes are represented), hard-working and loyal, though primitive, mountain people who physically look more like Polynesians or even Eskimos than Vietnamese. The remaining three companies are Vietnamese. I don't technically command this "battalion" (about 500 men), but my team actually advises a VNSF (sometimes known as LLDB, for Luc Luong Dac Biet, the Vietnamese name) team which in turn commands them. My counterpart, 1LT Lang, the VNSF A team leader, appreciates the Montagnards but reportedly cannot treat them decently for fear his conduct will be reported to higher HQ where the Montagnards are less appreciated. Hence he recruits as many Montagnards as he can, but usually uses them for coolie-type labor. Potentially, the Montagnards (sometimes affectionately abbreviated as "Yards") are the best soldiers in camp, but due to their lack of training, leadership, and proper employment they are now the worst company. The Vietnamese have traditionally treated them as outcasts (the VNAF supposedly used to bomb Yard villages at random when the people declined to come into VN hamlets), so that now a movement known as FULRO (an acronym based on the French name) has arisen, with the intent of rising against the South VN government and taking over most of the highlands as an independent state.

Apparently they have a decent amount of power, cohesion, and leadership, as I understand RVN Vice President Ky feels threatened enough to have conducted secret talks with FULRO leaders. This is played low key, of course, and is no real problem in my camp, but is bad in places near Cambodia where some VNSF tyrants reign and almost all CIDG troops are Yards. A friend of mine got into serious difficulty and was relieved from two A camps due to sympathy and accidental involvement with the FULRO movement. As I said, no real problems exist here if one doesn't mind some deviations from our usual etiquette standards; I do get a bit bewildered when some Montagnard tribeswoman comes up to me, squats, pulls up her skirt, and drops an offering at my feet. I don't know whether to be offended, or consider it a tribute of respect and admiration, to be smeared on my forehead as a gesture of acceptance. One of the many problems of an A team CO.

My counterpart, 1LT Lang, is about 45 years old, and the story is that he used to be a major back when the VNSF were Diem's "palace guard," was demoted to second lieutenant after the 1963 coup, and is gradually working his way back up the ladder.

The logistics situation here is a bit unusual, and, frankly, also a bit insufficient. Having been told at previous posts like Berlin that things were hard to get because everything was in Vietnam, and having read General [William C.] Westmoreland's justification for so many non-combat personnel to support combat troops logistically, I expected everything to be available in abundance. Such is not necessarily the case.

First of all, I have an operating fund under my personal control of about 3.5 million piastres monthly ($30,000), which sounds massive but from which I must pay my CIDG troops, laborers, clerks, interpreters, cooks, etc., buy food, and pay for some materials not available elsewhere. Incidentally, unlike the "unit fund"

**FitzGibbon with his Vietnamese Special Forces counterpart,
Lieutenant Lang, who later received promotion to captain.**
Daniel H. FitzGibbon

in conventional army units, this fund is fairly loose and could easily be abused if one were so inclined.

Secondly, equipment, weapons (mostly old M-2 carbines and 1919A6 .30 cal. machine guns), tiger suits (camouflage fatigues), ammo, etc., are provided by the C team at Pleiku, air-lifted onto my runway. This is a major problem area, in that the items are easily lost (the men, having no disciplinary restraints, sometimes desert with weapons and equipment), and I am assigned personal financial responsibility for the whole lot. Although I should be able to gain relief from responsibility for those lost or captured items, I still have the problem of replenishing stocks and outfitting/training new recruits. Unfortunately, the supply channels from Pleiku, storage/air movement procedures, etc., are slow and erratic and have kept me from obtaining these items. I now have 40 new recruits, but no uniforms for them. No ammo pouches are available; the only boots are size 5½ and size 12. Ammo is way too low for mortars, and not great for the other weapons—particularly considering training needs, operations, and camp defense reserves required. I have 13 vehicles, most of which are about 10–12 years old, my mechanics are poorly trained natives, and no repair parts (with a few exceptions) are readily available. These items have been requisitioned and re-requisitioned, but no relief is presently in sight. Building materials (cement, lumber, pierced steel plate, etc.) are hard to get, my fund is overdrawn $600 already in construction costs, and the camp is only about 60 percent completed in my estimation.

No post exchanges (PXs) are available to purchase cigarettes and toiletries, or any nice equipment (cameras, tape recorders) that I would like. Sundry packages are issued to conventional U.S. units in the field (complete with cigarettes, toiletries, etc.), but they are no longer issued to Special Forces units. We are also not issued food at all, and must fend for ourselves on that count. Fortunately, the artillery usually is able to draw extra rations, and my NCOs have acquired some generous sources in other U.S. units in Bong Son and other places, so we eat well enough. The trouble is that cigarettes must be purchased on the black market in Bong Son, at $3.00 a carton (they sell for $1.30 in the PX). Since they are rationed in the PX, however, only individuals with their own ration cards can purchase them, thereby precluding one of my team members who happens to be visiting a place with a PX from making group purchases for all of us. Most of the building material thus far used and nearly all of the remainder we get have been scrounged through First Cavalry Division supply points by exchanging captured weapons or similar items. Everything has its price, but it should be free, it should come through normal channels, and no private or sergeant in some logistical base should be getting money or trophies for issuing supplies.

The black market here is pretty blatant, but I don't blame the Vietnamese as much as the Americans for this fact. In the open, in most villages, are stands selling American cigarettes, toiletries, cameras, and government equipment that, except for occasional thefts and desertions, could only have been obtained from Americans running PXs and logistical bases. I sometimes have to use the black market to get things for my camp and my men, and again, it bothers me to do so since these things should be provided for free through regular supply lines.

As I said before, my counterpart, 1LT Lang, is the actual camp commander, though if the camp is overrun, an operation fails, innocent civilians are injured, or the camp defenses are inadequate or sloppy, my bosses will naturally hold me responsible. Thus I have to do my best to cause my counterpart to act as I would act if fully in charge. Convincing an experienced Vietnamese officer of tactical necessities, requirements to push field operations, etc., is often very difficult, but generally tact, patience, repetition, and imagination get the job done. I've learned to plant suggestions and raise questions indirectly so as to induce my counterpart to come up with my idea or position as his own. This can take time, but it certainly beats the unproductive standoff a couple of my predecessors often found themselves in. The important thing, as told to me by my bosses, is that good rapport and mutual respect be maintained to permit progress to be made toward our military and civil objectives, even if there are some tactical differences, unsafe situations, and even some suspected corruption involved. Some of my A team members think the VNSF pad payrolls and take kickbacks on jobs and even death benefits to next of kin, but they have no proof to back up their claims. If I find evidence of corruption, I won't be shy about reporting it, but right now my A team has too much other stuff to do to add criminal investigations to its responsibilities. So far, 1LT Lang and I have gotten along OK, and I think it's partly because I've avoided the corruption accusations and resulting animosity experienced by a couple of my predecessors. He listens to me, often takes my advice on operational issues, and generally is tactically competent. The other VNSF team members are questionable, but two (an intelligence sergeant and a medic) are supposed to be really capable and aggressive. While I often think it would be more efficient and effective if I were the commander, not 1LT Lang, I recognize that this type of war places emphasis on civil victories and not just military successes, so the Vietnamese government must direct the war themselves.

Some of my USASF team members claim the VNSF are not only corrupt but unwilling to go after the VC aggressively. They describe the attitude of the Vietnamese as: they're making money on this war, they don't want to chance getting killed or hurt, they've been fighting for years so don't expect to end it quickly, and they realize that if they delay long enough an American unit will move into the enemy's location and fight the battle for them. My teammates may be right, but I'll have to see for myself. I've become friends with one of our Vietnamese civilian interpreters, who says many Vietnamese distrust American motives and think we want to colonize Vietnam or make it our fifty-first state. They can't believe anyone would contribute so much money and lives just to be nice, and resent the fact we have so much wealth to give. As a result, they feel perfectly entitled to get all they can while they can. It's an interesting if strange perspective; the more generous we are and the less apparent our self-interest, the more they question our intentions. We think they should love us for our gifts, but they dislike and distrust us for our ability and willingness to make gifts. I wonder if the European recipients of Marshall Plan donations felt the same way.

Living conditions for my A team are pretty good—everything's relative, of course. If you've slept in foxholes or snow without protective blankets or sleeping bags, if you've bathed and shaved in cold mountain streams, and if you've defecated by digging a hole and leaning from a tree trunk, then anything's tolerable. I live in an underground bunker with my own room (about 10 ft. by 4 ft.), a cot with sheets and blankets, a small dresser and chair. We have constructed a wooden mess hall/bar, and the food we scrounge is tolerable. A cold shower/faucet is located higher up the hill, and an outdoor privy type latrine is nearby. We have hired a maid to wash our clothes, so we stay relatively clean.

The chain of command here is awkward, as you can imagine. As the American A team leader, I work for the U.S. B team at Qui Nhon, the camp is commanded by VNSF with a parallel VNSF B team at Qui Nhon, my camp and TAOR are in Hoai An District of Binh Dinh Province, so all actions must be cleared through district and province officials having their own State Department and military advisers. I'm under the U.S. Army First Field Force, Vietnam and II Corps Command area, and under operational control (for our patrols and other troop movements and combat actions) of whichever U.S. unit is in the area (was First Cavalry until all moved north to I Corps—now Fourth Infantry Division). Plans must be cleared through the Republic of Korea (ROK) Division and 173rd Airborne Brigade when they're in the area, and through USAF and VNAF when air is involved. My fire support comes from several different sources depending on type and my air and logistical support comes from others. The U.S. artillery battery next door occupies part of my camp's outer perimeter, and is under <u>my</u> operational control in the event the camp comes under attack. The artillery battery, however, has coordinating responsibility for my camp's mortars fired in support of our operations in the field. You need a scorecard to see who your boss is.

Binh Dinh Province is reportedly 60 percent pacified, but that leaves plenty which is not. It's also not especially comforting when you realize that the person assigning this estimate, which is heavily subjective, is the one responsible for pacifying the province. There is something inherently flawed in a system where progress is measured by the people responsible for accomplishing the progress and evaluated on how much progress is achieved. The province advisor measuring "pacification" is in exactly that position. Moreover, the short 12 month tours of duty of the province advisers are not designed to achieve lasting results and long-term accountability—you go in, find things in disarray, institute new measures, proclaim a success, and take off. Not to pick just on the province advisers; the same could be said for all or most of us. No wonder progress seems so elusive.

The camp's defensive situation is hardly to my liking at present, but we're making progress. With the camp under basic construction and with many of the troops committed to field operations, it's hard to do everything but some defensive measures need improvement. The alert procedure is outdated and inadequate, communications are weak or ineffective, no method or position exists for observing the area to determine the point of attack and direct mortar fire, there's only one row of Claymore mines and then over only part of the perimeter, no fougasse (electronically detonated barrels of gasoline, oil, and C-4 plastic explosive) is in place, barbed wire is inadequate and does not restrict movement through the heavily vegetated draws leading up to the camp, bunkers for machine guns are inadequate and some are placed in positions where firing won't do much good, no decent plan for evacuation or emergency helicopter pad exists, claymores are single primed so are half as reliable as they should be and are controlled from a position too far removed from the operations center, the CIDG mortar crews need a lot more training to fire properly, no reaction force exists within my inner perimeter, emergency communications equipment is faulty, etc., etc. *ad infinitum.* In general, the setup is questionable, although hopefully adequate for defense against a battalion-sized (500 men) attack; I doubt if it can stop a two regiment (1,500 men each) attack. We've really got to make some changes and soon.

My team has two intelligence nets operating in my TAOR, with the separate nets intended to provide independent reports and offer a possibility of confirmation. We also have a counter-intelligence net in the CIDG companies to detect VC infiltration if possible.

**FitzGibbon with two of his Civilian Irregular Defense Group
company commanders at Ha Tay.**
Daniel H. FitzGibbon

There are so many ways to hit this camp subversively that one can go berserk stopping all gaps, but things can improve. My TAOR is in the middle of a secure VC stronghold, used as HQ for the Third NVA Division, infiltration, and medical convalescence. Intelligence reports indicate at least 2½ regiments are within 10 miles of camp at all times. These reports far exceed my capacity to react with ground troops, so I often have to call for unobserved fire missions from the artillery to soften these areas. Many locations are underground in tunnels with concealed entrances, so you can imagine the difficulty of detecting and destroying them. My counterpart informed me that these tunnels were started at least 20 years before, and I believe him. I imagine that ¾ of South Vietnam has tunnels underground used for infiltration, hiding, and headquarters. We have received reports for several days that the NVA will attack this camp and have been openly telling the people this information. I don't necessarily believe all this but do expect a mortar attack in the near future. District HQ up the road has been mortared (two days ago) and other installations in the area have, but for some reason this camp has never been hit.

Contacts have been fairly heavy in the operations sent from camp. We have a requirement to maintain ⅓ to ½ of the camp strength in the field on operations. This is important if we are to find and attack the enemy, but it also keeps us from making the defensive improvements we need to make. My counterpart would rather keep the CIDG in camp, so I've really had to work hard to maintain the required force in the field. The weapons carried by the CIDG in these operations are not very adequate; machine guns and 60 mm mortars are left behind since they are "too heavy," leaving only the very light carbines of World War II vintage. 1LT Lang often sends only small platoon-sized (30 men) operations, usually three at a time, in separate directions, without

VNSF leadership, on which occasions I don't send my team members or myself to advise. A platoon is too small to effectively resist an attack, yet big enough to provide a lucrative target. In addition, without VNSF leadership and a U.S. presence, the CIDG are pretty unaccountable and don't accomplish much. So I prefer company-sized (130 or so men) or larger operations, with two VNSF and two USASF A team members (to watch out for and backup each other). Each operation goes for five to six days and returns, while another then departs. Operations lay ambushes, conduct search and clear operations, etc., and have had limited success. A seven-man ambush tonight knocked out two VC and wounded two others.

The weather here is presently mild with the monsoon season just ending—45 degrees at night and 80 degrees during the day. Fog hangs in the morning in the valleys. Mosquitoes are bad enough to warrant mosquito nets for beds and daily anti-malaria pills (in addition to the weekly Chloroquine-Primaquine capsules). It will warm up as we move into the dry season.

The poverty of the people is about as expected. Dusty roads, dried mud shacks, poor sanitation, bad food, rice paddies, etc. prevail. The average laborer makes about $20 per month. I try to do all I can for civil affairs projects. We're building a school, bridges, etc., and we've passed out seeds and taught the farmers how to grow vegetables. We treat about 200 people daily on medical patrols, and do all possible to improve sanitation and education in the area. I visit the villages fairly often and talk to the village chiefs and other elders. Most are friendly and appreciative of our help, having had frequent VC terrorist raids resulting in kidnappings, killings, and burned huts (several hundred were burned in a VC attack just before I arrived). I also go in big for psychological operations—plenty of leaflets after artillery strikes to VC, loudspeakers, safe-conduct passes, movies for CIDG and villagers, the whole bit. I actually think it helps.

Well, I've exhausted the pen for tonight. Now that you have my address, expect many letters. This one alone is several weeks' worth—I've divided it into parts for mailing purposes. Would also appreciate subscription to *The* [Columbus] *Republic* if you can oblige. Give my best to Nancy and Don—I guess they've about a week to go until their wedding. I'm sure Nancy is a nervous wreck by now. Tell her to write and send me some wedding pictures—I'll be thinking of her next Saturday.

Love,
Dan

---

9 March 1968

Dear Folks,

Have received two letters thus far—one dated 18 February arrived on 4 March—your fourth (my second received) dated 3 March arrived today. The package has not yet arrived. I imagine this is the first letter (your fourth) that was sent to my exact location—the others are between Company B and here. There are so many variables concerning mail—availability of aircraft included. Mail runs are usually combined with resupplies, VIP visits, or hot classified info.

Was real glad to hear your description of Nancy's wedding; it sounded very nice and I am sure you all were proud. That was funny about Nancy's veil, although I doubt if you thought so at the time. Also, pat the kids on the back for me for a good show—they must have been real cute. Tell Nancy and Don to write me when they get to Brussels, and I promise to reply.

I see Dad's ready for another birthday—still young and spry as ever I'm sure. I hope his birthday's a happy one and that he enjoys his special day. I'll be thinking of him on Saturday.

To continue with my "general orientation" of camp life at Ha Tay, I have ten fine soldiers working for me, which means I'm a little short-handed. I have an executive officer, lLT Mundhenk, who handles the finances, supplies, and administrative end of the workload to spare me for tactical operations. He's from Illinois, and seems like a bright, friendly, and capable guy. He arrived here about one week after I did, but he had experience at the nearby Vinh Thanh A camp for nine months. My civil affairs/psychological operations (CA/PO) officer, lLT Allen, a tall, lanky, energetic North Carolinian, is responsible for refugee support, medical assistance, schools, sanitation, playgrounds, farming, animal husbandry, etc. for the 3,000 villagers in my TAOR and several thousand in outlying villages as well. He also handles the psy ops (loudspeaker broadcasts, movies, leaflets, etc.) directed toward our CIDG troops, the villagers, and of course our good friend Charlie. He's very diligent and seems to enjoy his work. My operations/team sergeant, MSG Franco, a Mexican-American from Texas, acts as my first sergeant as far as supervising the enlisted men and running duty rosters is concerned. He's sort of gruff and blunt, and can sometimes be critical of the VNSF, my ambitious plans, and some of our fellow team members (who sometimes grumble about him, too), but he is a hard worker, an excellent soldier, and a straight shooter. His prime duty, as the title implies, is to keep tabs on all operations, messages, plans, artillery/air coordination, reports, and anything else that comes up. SFC Smith, who is very bright and has the manner of a professor, is the intelligence sergeant. He supervises the American intelligence and counter-intelligence nets, coordinates with VNSF on their nets, monitors all intelligence reports received from other agencies, briefs me daily on the current situation, and is responsible for security of information and documents. SFC Grau is my light weapons sergeant, responsible for allocation, maintenance, and control of all small arms (up to but not including recoilless rifles and mortars), and for training the CIDG in firing them. He also distributes, monitors, and requisitions ammunition for these weapons. He's a tough, straight, hard-working soldier who looks like he stepped out of a Special Forces recruiting poster. SFC Parker, a big, strong, black sergeant from North Carolina, just arrived today to take over the heavy weapons. He has the same responsibilities for mortars and recoilless rifles, plus he prepares the indirect fire defense plan for the camp in coordination with supporting artillery units. He seems very good and conscientious. Both of the weapons men, of course, have a major role in determining which bunkers are built where for which weapons, and for coordinating their fire if attacked (final protective lines, barrages, etc., providing a "wall of steel" throughout the perimeter). SFC Parker replaces SFC DeLeon, a native of Guam who departed last week to take an operations sergeant slot in another camp. My senior engineer departed today, leaving only one engineer/demolitions expert for the present, SP5 Spaulding. Spaulding does the supervising on all construction and the preparation of barriers. He has his work cut out for him, but knows this and appears hardworking, innovative and serious; he will be the key to a successful camp defense. Our communications expert, SSG Roese, is responsible for operating our many and varied radios (including continuous wave Morse Code), checking the telephone/radio nets for camp defense, constructing and maintaining antennas (we have about 10), supervising our generator and electrical wiring status, and maintaining, stocking, controlling, and requisitioning all communications equipment. He becomes sort of an operations sergeant out of necessity in view of his requirement for knowing all about operations and serves as an artillery coordinator in many cases. Right now he has no assistant since his last one was transferred about a week ago, and believe me this is as frustrating and exhausting a job as there is. Thank goodness Roese is as good as they come and has a positive, dedicated attitude. He spends virtually all of his time in the Commo Room without relief, but calls people "Good Buddy" on the radio and always has a cheerful smile. I have two medics, SGT Daniel, a small, friendly, and intelligent black man from Los Angeles, and SP4 Petersen, a less experienced white man from Minnesota who seems bright and eager to learn; they work well as a team and do an awful lot. They check camp sanitation (always a problem), give exams to food handlers, analyze the drinking water, treat civilian, CIDG, and U.S. casualties (battle or otherwise), give numerous shots, deliver babies, arrange for medical evacuation, go into villages to treat diseases (they averaged 1,000 persons treated monthly on these medical patrols—I've encouraged them to expand these patrols, and they have treated 800 thus far in March), and generally do a lot of good. SF medics are the best non-professional medics in the world—they can even perform amputations and limited surgery. This then is my team. Most are outstanding and all appear to be very capable and conscientious.

All of the members of my A team go on operations (even the medics, who are classed as combatants and do not wear red crosses). Since one of the easiest ways to take this camp is to infiltrate the inner perimeter and shoot up the Americans, an American is always awake and on duty observing the area. All of us pull this guard duty (including me) for three hours (midnight to

3:00 a.m. or 3:00 a.m. to 6:00 a.m.) about once every three or four days, since two or three of the men are usually gone on operations.

The weather here is quite warm—not too hot and humid but enough so that I have a nice tan already. The monsoon season in this part of Vietnam (as I may have mentioned) is supposed to end this month and start again in November, but last season was light and we have had rain only slightly since my arrival.

I normally maintain three guerrilla operations in the field at all times—hitting the VC with their own techniques. Each operation lasts about five days and I send two American advisers with each company-sized operation (most operations are just platoon-sized). In addition to these, I send the recon platoons out when I can talk my counterpart into it to check out intelligence reports and lay ambushes in areas of enemy movement patterns. Finally, three outposts are maintained on the high spots around the camp (within 800 mcters), each with 10–15 men who rotate after seven days. I have little confidence in them, since many of the men sleep too much, they all cluster together instead of spacing out (leaving wide gaps for VC infiltration), and the VNSF rarely inspects them to straighten them out. Since the First Cavalry Division moved north to I Corps, the First Battalion, Thirty-fifth Infantry, of the Third Brigade, Fourth Infantry Division (1/35/3/4 if you prefer) is responsible for the area of which my TAOR is a part, so we plan to conduct joint operations in the near future. Right now they have a company in my TAOR to the northwest of camp (making me a bit nervous since I have a platoon without Americans in the area and they look too much like VC). I have a company plus to the southeast in the valley known as the 506 valley—a real hot area named after the closed dirt highway running through—with 1LT Allen and SGT Daniel. They killed eight VC today and captured 15 VC suspects/sympathizers, at the loss of no CIDG. A good

ratio, I believe. I have not gone on any of these extended operations yet (just small forays around camp) but plan to take the next
company out. I've thus far been too busy getting organized to take
off for a week. I plan to go out on more, and more hazardous,
operations than my team members to set a good example.

We're still waiting to get hit by mortars and/or ground attack
on the camp. Intelligence predicted a hit on or before 6 March—
since nothing happened the forecast is extended to 31 March. I'm
not worried about it, although I am pushing barrier construction
as quickly as possible. District HQ (about 8–10 km to the north)
and police HQ (next door to it) were scheduled to be hit and were
hit, but we are among the uninitiated thus far. The enemy buildup
continues to be heavy around here. Recent reports of increased
infiltration into CIDG ranks led us to create an internal security
counter-intelligence net that succeeded in rooting out three VC
suspects from my troops and implicating two others. My friendly
counterpart turned them over to the National Police instead of
interrogating them thoroughly and processing them through
Special Forces channels as I had advised.

One of my major chores here is coordinating artillery fire in the
area and directing air strikes on known/suspected enemy locations.
Since our ability to react to intelligence reports is limited (my counterpart won't use the recon platoons as much as I want to), we are
blessed to have considerable artillery support to direct fire upon suspected VC locations. We have several batteries of 8 inch howitzers,
175 mm guns, 105 howitzers, Dusters, etc., more or less at my disposal, so I try to take full advantage of them. Aircraft are sometimes
available for reconning and assessing damage, and of course for conducting air strikes on the most lucrative and entrenched targets.

One thing I should emphasize is the care taken to preserve civilian lives in the conduct of military operations. Never before, as far

An 81 mm mortar pit at Ha Tay.
Daniel H. FitzGibbon

as I'm aware, have military commanders gone to such extremes to protect civilians at the expense of lucrative targets and even to the extent of placing military lives in jeopardy. The Vietnamese district and province civilian officials have given us an overlay of areas which are off-limits to civilians and which are classed as Free Fire Zones for all weapons, artillery, and air strikes. Even within these areas, no persons are fired upon unless their locations are confirmed, their identity is proven hostile (uniforms and/or weapons), and they cannot possibly be plain old civilians. The above restrictions are American— the Vietnamese say "fire away." Air strikes (to include napalm) must be approved by II Corps and all civilian officials in the chain—they are never called for on inhabited villages unless an Allied Force is in heavy contact there and the village is in the Free Fire Zone. (All villagers in Free Fire Zones have been notified of such and been told to move previously—the Vietnamese officials assume the ones who stay are VC or VC supporters.) Napalm is extremely rare. No one in my camp has ever seen it used, and the only cases I've heard of are in forests and mountainsides where only VC could possibly be. The amount of medical aid, refugee support, and other aid given by Americans is unparalleled and sincere (although I'm told there have been cases in other camp areas where, unbeknownst to the Americans, the village chief has stood outside the medical aid tent charging patients 50 piastres to be treated or where the Vietnamese school teachers charge their students for the free school kits, paper, pencils, and textbooks given by the U.S.), and full restitution is given for any accidental crop or animal destruction. I used to get the idea that, although bombings were controlled, they were frequent and napalm was widespread and almost indiscriminate, but such is surely not the case. It's a shame few Americans realize this.

Every once in a while the Vietcong attack the friendly nearby villages where no soldiers are stationed, killing or kidnapping the

Tran Ke Thien, known as Jack, served as FitzGibbon's principal interpreter while at Ha Tay.
Daniel H. FitzGibbon

village chiefs and other civilians and burning the huts where the people live. It's a real setback to our efforts to establish civil government and give the people a sense of comfort in relying on our troops for protection. We occasionally put troops in the villages and on ambush positions leading into the villages overnight, and I recently led an operation that did that without success. The village of Vinh Hoa, located just west across the river, has a reputation for being a VC village because when all the other villages are attacked it is always unscathed. The people also seem hostile when we visit them. Our belief is that they support the VC, providing food and intelligence to them, but there is no way we can prove that fact.

My Vietnamese is improving daily but I still use an interpreter when I talk with my counterpart. He talks too fast and uses too many new words for me to make it by myself, but I think I do pretty well getting my point across to him (using my own words and at my own pace).

I have been plagued here recently by many VIP visits although my boss hasn't made it here yet. Some were bigwigs from the Fourth Infantry Division moving in to get acquainted, some were artillery brass coordinating with the battery next door, some were Vietnamese wheels, and some I'm convinced were just taking a break from their desk jobs. Maj. Gen. [William R.] Peers, the First Field Force Commanding General, who is scheduled for his third star momentarily, spent an afternoon with me and seemed pleased with what he saw. Each of these visitors has to be briefed, toured, and fed coffee, none of which is hard but all of which is time-consuming.

Don't get the idea I have it rough in terms of living conditions here. Compared to many infantry troopers who return to base camp only about half the time, I have it pretty soft. Of course there have been some times when I wish I was commanding an American infantry company instead of advising VNSF on some civilian irregular troops.

Construction here goes on as usual. I have established priorities for construction projects and added quite a few, so my engineer will have his hands full for a while. We have employed 55 civilian laborers to do the construction work on the inner perimeter—the CIDG does the work on the outside. This is a bone of contention between 1LT Lang and myself—I want the CIDG to do more work and more quickly and he wants laborers to do the work on the outside. He has his reasons, but until the inside is done cold the CIDG will have to do the outside or it won't get done. Holding the purse strings is a definite negotiating advantage.

Sanitation here is a big problem. Although we've succeeded in getting latrines dug, many of the Vietnamese prefer the nearest dry spot when opportunity knocks. Trash is dumped at random, although a trash dump is located outside the camp and I have been pushing my counterpart for a trash bin inside camp to supplement it. One result of the sanitation problem is an excessive number of rats permeating the place and running free. Although no plague exists yet, this disease is feasible as long as the rats run free. As I write this letter, rats are scurrying across my ceiling and on the walls. They are in the mess hall, supply building, and about everywhere. They won't eat the rat poison, so it's ineffective. What we need is about 30 cats, I suppose. Until then I'll have to keep racking my brain and pushing my counterpart to clean the place up.

I have enclosed a couple of pictures of myself taken with the detachment Polaroid. These are the "ruined" shots of an attempt to get a decent photo for my B team's rogues' gallery. As you can see, I have no talented photographers in the detachment.

Two Polaroid snapshots of FitzGibbon he sent to his family from Ha Tay.
Daniel H. FitzGibbon

Well, that's about it for now, at last. I hope eventually to settle into a routine whereby I relate the day's activities each night and combine to send a week's news at a time. Right now I'm still getting organized plus trying to explain some general things which are really not suited to a diary-type affair.

Take care of yourselves, give my best to Nancy and Don and Happy Birthday again, Dad.

Love,
Dan

---

11 March 1968

Dear Folks,

Starting out a regular journal, now that things are pretty well organized.

The last two days I have been wrapped up in the operation 1LT Allen and SGT Daniel are advising to the southeast of here about 5 km in the 506 valley. Saturday afternoon, while rummaging through the immense network of tunnels, bunkers, etc., they encountered a company of NVA and opened fire. They killed eight enemy and captured two prisoners and two weapons, suffering two CIDG slightly wounded by punji stakes (bamboo poles sharpened to razor edge, dipped in dung, and planted in concealed holes). This operation continued to find trouble when an NVA company of 100 men attacked their position about 3:00 a.m. Sunday. This time they killed at least two VC/NVA, but lost two CIDG killed and five wounded. This continued for about two hours, during which time we had continuous illuminations from artillery and 4.2 inch mortars, as well as the heavy high explosive stuff. These artillery boys are really great—they fire round after round all night in support of operations and on enemy troop concentrations identified through my intelligence nets. We tried to get a helicopter with parachute flares (flare ship) and a heavily armed helicopter (gunship) or two to help out, but the fog runs so thick that when the flare ship took off it crashed, killing all four Americans aboard—a real shame.

The operation also picked up about 30 civilians for detention, which we brought back by chopper after the daylight finally came. These civilians live in an area restricted from habitation and have been told to move or be fired upon, but still live there. There were about 10 women of different ages, about 20 small children and babies, and one old man. Either the fathers of these children are VC on operation or the old man is more virile than he appears. Four of the women turned out to be hard-core VC workers—the rest just helped the VC to avoid being shot by them. Of the two prisoners captured, one was a boy about 13 years old (hardest-looking of the lot), and the other was shot while trying to escape.

Contact continued sporadically through Sunday (it rained all day and the fog was quite thick). One of the Forward Air Controllers (FACs), Ben Glawe, who is probably as daring as any of them, usually gets shot at when he goes up, and makes me airsick whenever I fly with him, came on in despite the weather and reconned Lt. Allen's operation as it moved along Sunday PM. They hit a squad, but got no casualties.

They pulled in about 1800 (6:00 p.m.) after going all day and set up a quick perimeter around their position (trip flares, claymores, etc.). About 2100 (9:00 p.m.) they got hit by a company

**FitzGibbon prepares to board an O-1 with U.S. Air Force Captain Ben Glawe
for a reconnaissance mission around Ha Tay.**
Daniel H. FitzGibbon

(apparently a probing attack only), but detected them early and think they got a few (any bodies were dragged off by the VC so no kills were credited). Once again, artillery and illumination were responsive and accurate, and flare ships wouldn't even move unless we were in desperate shape after their experience of the previous night. They never got hit again, except for minor sniper fire the rest of the night, although I expected something big and had him shift machine-gun positions.

The two dead CIDG were brought in Sunday AM, and placed in the dispensary (obviously this is rather tough on the morale of the wounded, but until we can build a regular funeral house it's the only place to put them). Their relatives, friends, and professional mourners gathered where they burned incense and candles, cried, sang songs, and wailed, making one hellacious racket all morning until we boxed the bodies up and sent them to their relatives' houses.

Today has been relatively quiet. The weather is bright and sunny, so Charlie has retired until evening. The operation is resting and plans to set out ambushes in the village areas about 3–4 km north of camp. I have a FAC in the air above them now providing help.

Every Monday morning at 8:00 a.m. we hold a formation of troops, at which the flag is raised and the RVN national anthem is sung. My counterpart and I stand out in front. I always wonder if Charlie will figure out our routine and lob some mortar rounds into our massed formation. Everyone salutes the flag as it is raised. The U.S. flag isn't permitted to be raised in this camp, but apparently that's customary everywhere. I do have one on the wall in my TOC.

We have another company operation going out Thursday at 6:00 a.m. for five days into a large area covering about 8 km north and 6 km west of camp in a square shape. Much of it is in villages that have been pacified but which are now being harassed by the VC (the infrastructure is trying to take over). I plan on taking this operation with MSG Franco. Two other smaller platoon-sized operations, without Americans, will move to the south and west respectively.

It is now Wednesday night. Not a whole lot has happened since then but I've been busy enough anyway. The operation with 1LT Allen and SGT Daniel continued through Tuesday night but encountered no more VC. They did hit an extensive mine/booby trap field, wounding four men (two seriously) on one mine even though they had sent some "VC" cows through ahead to clear the area.

We had a B-52 strike (these are really hard to come by) in the south of my TAOR on Tuesday evening, followed by a Long Range Reconnaissance Patrol (LRRP) team assessment. Although I haven't yet received the assessment report, I imagine the damage was extensive and the bunkers in that area destroyed.

I've been working on a plan for the 506 valley, a big grandiose scheme which, if no word leaks out, could do some decent damage. The general plan is to notify the people living in the villages there illegally that they must move out or their houses will be destroyed (they have been told that before—the area is a Free Fire Zone—now these people seem to be supporting the VC and providing intelligence for them). Several similar areas away from the 506 will be notified as well, in order to divert attention from the 506 as a specific target area. A B-52 strike will hit the most extensive tunnels and bunkers in the area (east side of valley), but we may have to settle for lighter aircraft. A LRRP will assess the place, then I'll move in with seven companies (two of my CIDG, three from other camps, and two U.S. infantry companies) to assume blocking positions and sweep across the valley. I think it's a good plan and ought to work, particularly with the way the maneuver companies' axes of advance and the positions of the blocking forces (eight of them) would seal off the valley. A leaflet drop would terminate the operation. This should, if combined with burning of village huts, alleviate our problem in this area. My plan has been approved in concept by my VNSF counterpart, district officials, and the Third Brigade, Fourth Infantry Division CO (we're under his operational control and would have to get the two companies and helicopters from him). My boss at B team should approve, since he recognizes this as the hottest area in eastern II corps, but the boys at the top will have to weigh priorities when it comes to the B-52 aspect.

I'm all set to move out on my operation tomorrow for five days. I expect to encounter some mines and booby traps, and perhaps a company of local force VC, but nothing too serious. My counterpart has elected to join me, so I'm happy about that.

Well, gotta close and get packing.

Love,
Dan

---

28 March 1968

Dear Folks,

Your letters are starting to come in regularly about six or seven days after postmarked. The newspapers started about two weeks ago for 5 March—each arrives about two weeks late and is enjoyable to receive. I also got a package on 17 March from you which contained toiletries, a book, Life Savers, etc., and your copies of newspapers. Those packages are just perfect—I still haven't been able to get from here to a PX where I can buy toiletries so everything you had was ideal. If you can send one such package once a month I should be well supplied, and if it's not asking too much you might throw in some more Tums, some cinnamon balls, and some after-shave lotion. These are really handy.

I went on my operation on 14 March and it turned out to be 7 days long instead of 5 as planned—it was generally a waste in my mind. I moved out at 0530 to the west (down a road where I was concerned we could easily be ambushed) with a company of CIDG, MSG Franco, and an artillery forward observer team of a lieutenant and a sergeant. I was pleased that 1LT Lang decided to come along—his first operation in about 7 months from what I hear. The purpose of this initial operation was to see if we could find and attack the VC believed to be based in the hills on the far side of Vinh Hoa by approaching them from the back. To do this, we had to climb up and down a number of mountains to get into the proper position. We first crossed the Kim Son River (wading through waist-high water), then headed north into the mountains. After securing a position on top of a mountain we sent out ambushes along VC trails we had spotted earlier. One lone VC walked into one and didn't last long. At the sound of the fire I moved over to the ambush site—it sounded like at least a platoon had hit with all the shooting. One of the worst things about being in a small unit combat situation, particularly in dense vegetation, is knowing what is going on. You hear gunfire and explosions and don't know who is attacking whom or in what numbers, let alone what else is out there waiting for you. One CIDG immediately tossed off an M-79 grenade launcher round in the general direction of the firing without being able to see anything in the thick foliage, so this naturally would make one uneasy. We didn't get probed, so moved farther north the next day, dodging a few mines and booby traps along the way.

Moving down a streambed we encountered a VC sentry and got him, then ran into the hut he was supposed to secure. About 20 people must have just left, as about that much room was available and that much cooked rice and clothes were around. We got a lot of documents showing names, letters, propaganda leaflets, and a few other things, but nothing of immediate tactical value. We then moved up from the streambed draw to a ridgeline (at my suggestion for security) and found several more bunkers. All huts, etc. were burned. We wandered around some more but found nothing really significant. We stayed on another hill that night and got a few stray mortar rounds but nothing close. The second morning out I impressed my troops while climbing up one mountain by throwing up along the path, thus delaying the operation by a few minutes while I tried to recover my health and my dignity. A combination of too much heat and humidity and no breakfast was apparently too much for me. In any case, I continued on. That night, reminding us that we were still at the tail end of the rainy season, the rain started to pour down on our location overnight (LON). We usually bring along hammocks to sleep in, even though there is a greater risk of getting hit by a bullet or shell fragments than when sleeping on the ground, simply because the ground is too hard and/or muddy to sleep comfortably. With the rainy night, the hammock helped a little, although even with a poncho overhead the soaking rain made it difficult to sleep. The rain continued on for another day and a half, by which time we felt pretty miserable.

When we finally did make it around to the location where we anticipated finding VC troops, we did come across a group of 15 to 20 men going through a village on the far side of the rice paddy from us. We opened fire on them, which they returned, hitting a CIDG troop standing next to me. We had no artillery or other support available to us, so by the time we crossed the rice paddy and got to the village where they had been there was no sign of them. They seemed to have gone into a tunnel in that area, but we could not find any opening. All in all, not a lot was accomplished, except to let the VC know that they would not be safe sitting in the hills on the far side of Vinh Hoa.

Incidentally, I've found I can go all day in this heat and humidity, refilling my canteen numerous times, without ever having to urinate. We fill our canteens in the rivers and streams when we cross them, purifying the water with tiny iodine tablets which turn the water into an unappetizing purple color if you look at it so I don't. I hope the iodine is strong, since on this last operation we refilled our canteens downstream from a location where we later found a body floating.

Back to the operation, the next morning I got a call to take my counterpart, prepare an LZ (landing zone) for a chopper, and move to a briefing from the Third Brigade, Fourth Infantry Division. Since no cleared area was near, we hacked out an LZ about 30 x 30 meters. The briefing concerned a plan of the Third Brigade to conduct a diversionary operation in the 506 as a decoy for a major operation they were mounting to the south of my TAOR. The 506 operation would consist of one CIDG company moving through on armored personnel carriers (APCs) supported by tanks, checking out the draws and ridgelines off the 506. I was opposed to the plan because I thought the tanks and APCs would move too slowly and loudly through the rice paddies, stream, and thickets to catch anyone, no blocking forces were available to seal off withdrawal routes, and the plan would scare off the VC/NVA from the area I was hoping to lure them into for my big operation to take place shortly thereafter. Since I'm under the operational control of the Third Brigade, of course, my opinion didn't matter a whole lot and I was overruled. I felt better later when I found that their big operation to the south, which was more important than my plan for the 506, had no contact with the VC/NVA.

So, I moved back, picked up the CIDG company I was with, and we returned toward camp in preparation for the change in plan and direction. En route to camp we caught a VC sentry, but did not find what he was guarding.

We stayed that night in a village north of camp, moved back the following morning, and hopped on the APCs to move out down the 506. The plan was to make a thrust into the 506 as far as possible the first day in case the VC decided to hit us heavily with mines or rockets, then move back slowly, checking out the draws, streambeds, and ridgelines on the sides of the valley. I moved out sitting on top of an APC—having been told that in case we hit a mine my chances of survival were greater if I was not inside the APC. After plodding along slowly, having to use an armored vehicle landing bridge (AVLB) to spread across some streambeds, the APC I was riding on flipped over into a ditch. Yours truly executed a one-and-one-half gainer, ending up on my head in the ditch. Nobody was really hurt, and although I was stunned momentarily, cut up my forehead, and had a monstrous stiff neck for about a week, I was OK. Needless to say, I continued on the operation with few problems, although I can't remember what I said for the rest of the day. It must have been adequate, though, because we corralled 180 detainees, burned several illegal villages, and discovered quite a few tunnels and bunkers although no VC. I may sound hard regarding those detainees and their villages, but they have been told countless times to move out, have been taken out before and returned, provide support and intelligence for the VC, and since my friendly counterpart wanted to shoot them all I think they got off lighter than they could have. They were taken to camp, interrogated, and sent to district HQ for relocation. Nothing much happened in the 506 valley, as I expected, except that we did search the area pretty thoroughly, killed only one more VC, and captured two others.

I was left with mixed impressions of the CIDG when I returned on the 21st. On the one hand, they are hard workers, courageous and plodding, with instinctive knowledge when VC or booby traps are in the area, but on the other hand many are undisciplined, will avoid contact unless pushed, are careless, and prefer to chase down pigs and chickens for food when we enter the villages instead of looking for VC, weapons, caches, documents, etc. Most of the problem, I've concluded, is in the leadership and example set by the LLDB (VNSF). When the LLDB push them, they do well, but when allowed to cool it will proceed to do so.

While I was on the operation two things big broke in camp. One was an apparent plague epidemic in a village about 6 km north of here out of my TAOR (Khoa Truong), caused by rats and believed transported in by VC further NW of here. That may be giving the VC more credit than they deserve. Anyway, the plague was discovered by my medic in one of his medical action patrols (medcaps)—no one would come in to report it in spite of our promptings, probably because they were terrified of the VC who had previously burned the village. Some villagers were already dead when the plague was discovered, and others died later. We had a team come in to help inoculate everyone and sterilize the area, but this should not have been necessary.

The second thing was that the temporary civilian laborers used for camp construction were cut out, putting a big damper on my plans to fix everything up here. I will have to use CIDG instead, with dubious results expected. The thing that bothers me is that my camp was allotted only $10,000 to build this camp, while two new camps are reportedly getting $25,000 each. One reason for this is may be that my camp is expected to be transferred to ARVN before too long, but this is indefinite and it won't help us in the meantime.

Love,
Dan

---

30 March 1968

Dear Folks,

Just got a chance to continue with my discourse—things have been rather hectic the last couple of days as you'll see later.

Upon my return, things started moving on my plan for operation in the 506. Operational control of the exercise was granted to the First Battalion, Thirty-fifth Infantry of the Fourth Infantry Division, making things a little difficult from my angle. It was decided to send two companies from my camp and two from other camps into the east side of the valley, one from another camp (Vinh Thanh) as reserve, two U.S. companies as blocking forces on the west side (on hills, instead of in the draws and streambeds as I had planned, thereby leaving gaps where the VC could withdraw quite easily, but less risk of ambush), one armored cavalry troop at the mouth of the valley, and two Popular Forces (National Guard type) platoons to "seal off" the north end of the valley. I had to organize, brief, and direct the CIDG elements, and insure the airlift of the units went smoothly. The operations actually accomplished very little with only five NVA killed and 21 detainees brought in, but many bunkers (180) were found with lots of equipment, documents, nice hospital equipment, and signs of recent habitation. I feel that the buildup of companies here at Ha Tay prior to the operation (instead of at a nearby staging area), the recent armored cavalry operation in the 506, and VC links within this camp compromised the plan, and the inability of the U.S. companies to seal off the draws completely at night probably let a few sneak by. Anyway, lessons learned for next time.

The Third Brigade has now moved out of the area, leaving the 173rd Airborne Brigade in its place, so I have been going through a round of meetings, briefings, etc. with all of these new people. The Third Battalion, 503rd Infantry from that brigade has set up HQ, a 105 howitzer battery, and a rifle company across the runway from me so things are moving quite well. The Vinh Thanh CIDG Company is still in the camp temporarily from the 506 operation.

Yesterday morning at about 8:45 I was briefing the C.O. of the 3/503 Infantry when I heard small arms and automatic weapons fire from nearby within the compound. Thinking we were under attack by a VC suicide squad of infiltrators, I grabbed my M-16 and moved out to check it out. The first thing I saw was 1LT Lang being carried up into my TOC, so I had one of my medics look after him while I moved down to the sound of the fighting to check it out, grabbing my chief interpreter as I went. I found out that no VC were in the camp (no more than usual, that is), but that my 516 Company (the best in camp) was shooting it out with the company from Vinh Thanh. Observing that no other USASF or LLDB were in the area, and afraid the battle would continue indefinitely until one side was annihilated and/or other units moved into action, and seeing no other course of action available, I grabbed a towel and moved into the crowd, me waving frantically and my interpreter shouting to cease fire. When the CIDG saw me they quit shooting and turned their rifles away. I spent another 15 minutes getting them separated and the Vinh Thanh Company moved out of camp and across the runway, with the help of the other USASF team members and a couple of VNSF from B team who happened to come by later. My people called medical evacuation choppers for the wounded and carried them to the dispensary. The final toll was two killed and 10 wounded from Vinh Thanh, and eight wounded from Ha Tay (including my counterpart). This apparently started because the Vinh Thanh Company, which had stayed back in reserve during the 506 operation, allegedly stole some stuff from Ha Tay's 516 Company's bunkers and harassed their dependents in the CIDG village nearby, so the 516 Company commander notified my counterpart that he planned to attack the Vinh Thanh Company. 1LT Lang just told him to forget it and said he'd check into it, then went down later to check it out; that was when the firing started. 1LT Lang wasn't wounded too seriously, but should be out for a month or two, during which time I hope to continue with the VNSF B team executive officer (a captain who seems to be pretty good) as acting camp commander. Just another example of the fun and games one can expect with the friendly CIDG—never a dull moment. Also, another way of many over here whereby one can get knocked off without really trying. One of the bad things about this, aside from the senseless loss of people, is that the 516 Company commander is the best CIDG soldier and leader in camp, and he will undoubtedly be tried for murder since he was arrested. A real shame, on all counts.

Well, just finished an extensive report on the incident and also my monthly operations summary. Beginning to get a little punchy around here, so may take off for Qui Nhon for a few days soon to get some rest and see my counterpart in the hospital there.

Keep the letters and packages coming—all are appreciated—and take care of yourselves.

Love,
Dan

---

7 April 1968

Dear Folks,

Just a quick note this time to let you know I'm OK. I have to go on another operation tomorrow (five days) to the south end of the 506 valley. I'm bringing a company of CIDG plus one of my recon platoons, and will check out the hospital, bunker, and tunnel complexes discovered on the big multi-company operation conducted two weeks ago. My intelligence reports show the VC are back in the area, rebuilding what we destroyed and re-inhabiting those bunkers we had to leave alone because the First Battalion, Thirty-fifth Infantry did not destroy them. The air strike I requested is still pending, so I expect to encounter a good bit of contact. It may sound strange, but I actually look forward to these operations, not only because it provides a chance to get away but also because of a weird feeling of "competition" and excitement involved. I haven't been too scared yet, but then I haven't really been involved in too much activity yet either.

When I go out on these operations, and periodically in camp, I eat with the CIDG and surprisingly enough enjoy most of the food. I've eaten much rice, which when mixed with shrimp, mushrooms, bouillon cubes, leaves, vegetables, etc. is very good. I've also eaten rice balls, rice bread, crayfish, crab, monkey, and other delicacies, served with fermented fish sauce. On these operations we eat captured cows and pigs, so I'm expecting some dysentery soon. I have yet to taste the real delicacies (boiled blood, duck heads, monkey brains, etc.) but suppose I will at least try it when confronted therewith. We sometimes eat American C Rations, but my favorite is the dried food (called LRRP rations, for long range recon patrol) to which you simply add hot water. I heat the water by burning a plastic explosive (C-4), which does not give out smoke and reveal our position.

My recent activity has been hectic in terms of adjusting to the requirements of the 173rd Airborne Brigade. They have elaborate reporting requirements, and feel that the CIDG (all of them) should be away from camp at all times. I think I'm doing well if I can get my counterpart to meet the new Fifth Special Forces Group requirement of 50 percent out on operations at any one time. The 173rd obviously doesn't understand that the CIDG have camp construction and defense duties and must be given some time off or they will desert. Unlike with U.S. troops, there is no disciplinary jurisdiction over them, nor a maximum of one-year tour for them.

The Third Battalion, 503rd Infantry, of that brigade was set up outside my camp for about two weeks but just left. With them, the artillery battery, and my crew, things were crowded, and I longed for the quiet and solitude of some isolated camp. Still, the other units make the camp a lot more secure than it would be without them.

We wear our regular army fatigues and green berets around camp, but wear camouflage uniforms and flop hats while on operations. The idea is to make us blend in with the CIDG troops, but our height and our inevitable proximity to the radio man make that difficult. I usually carry an M-16 rifle with me, although occasionally I carry a submachine gun in our arsenal since it is less cumbersome to carry around. I don't like being too encumbered on operations and need to keep my hands free to direct troops, use the radio, read the map, etc.; I'm not out there to supply firepower.

Nels Marin, an old friend from Berlin who's in S-1 at Fifth Special Forces Group HQ, stopped by on a visit and just left after four days. He's getting me a camera (his discretion) and will send it to me, so things should be improving in the photography line.

I am trying to take the Law School Admissions Test (LSAT) in August, to be administered in Nha Trang. I've sent away for a prep book, so shouldn't have any trouble. Perhaps the peace moves will help get me out in time for law school in September 1969 as hoped, but I can't see either side budging (at least not Hanoi) right now.

1LT Lang is improved and should be back in about a week, which is not all good news. His acting replacement, the VNSF B team executive officer, is really a sharp cookie and quite helpful.

Well, must close for now. Have received a letter from Nancy and four packages from you since my last letter. Thanks very much and the entire A team liked the cookies.

Love,
Dan

---

21 April 1968

Dear Folks,

I'm afraid my nicely planned system of writing daily notes and compiling them weekly for mailing has fallen down, but I'll try to keep you posted as regularly as possible.

When Nels went back to Nha Trang, he sent me an application form for the LSAT, which I promptly filled out and mailed. The test will be August 3rd, and since Nha Trang is an authorized test center, I will take it there. I've also sent for a preparation booklet. I asked that test scores be forwarded to IU, Michigan, Yale, Harvard, Texas, and Hastings, but will delay application to law schools (I think I'll apply to two or three to see where I can be accepted and what, if any, scholarships I can get) until November or so when I hope to have a better idea as to when I can get out of the army. Nels also sent me my W-2 forms (now I can't find my savings interest statements) so I suppose I'll go ahead and send in my tax form. I don't have to fill it out until 180 days after I return from VN.

I trust all is going well at home. I got a letter from Nancy while she was in Akron, Pa., but don't know her new address, so will write and mail to you for further forwarding to her new address when you get it.

After I last wrote I went on a four-day operation in the 506 valley with SFC Grau, my light weapons sergeant. The VNSF leader was a SGT Binh, their intelligence sergeant and a real outstanding soldier/leader. He likes to attract the VC, knowing that's the only way often to get contact, and I like his aggressive attitude. We succeeded, as we tumbled onto a hospital complex, ran across a small VC patrol and killed two of them, got probed or attacked every night, moved at night from one position to another, spotted a large VC ambush and scattered them with artillery, set up our own ambush and killed 5 NVA (my guess is they were the advance party for a larger unit—three of the five NVA were killed about 5 meters from me—each was speaking with North VN dialect and saying "don't shoot, we're your buddies from Hanoi," thinking we were the VC ambush we'd just busted up—one CIDG next to me was killed and one more wounded), getting sniped at, encountering

Sergeant Binh, the Vietnamese Special Forces intelligence specialist at Ha Tay.
Daniel H. FitzGibbon

more VC/NVA patrols and getting probed again, all in all having a real good time. Although we got a lot of contact, we only got the 7 VC/NVA killed, although blood trails were found indicating the enemy bodies and wounded were dragged away. The one night when we busted up the ambush and caught part of a company in our own, the artillery battery fired several hundred rounds, so I think we undoubtedly got quite a few more. I actually kind of enjoy these operations and don't mind the contact, not being especially nervous (although excited, admittedly), particularly with SFC Grau and a VNSF like SGT Binh along. SGT Binh was wounded, incidentally, a few days later on a night ambush with one of our reconnaissance platoons, but is recuperating well.

When I say that I wasn't especially nervous, I should emphasize that I was definitely excited and that my heart was beating swiftly. The point is that I simply had too much to do to allow myself the luxury of fear, as I had to control the troops on the ground, report by radio what was going on, and, where appropriate, call in artillery and/or air strikes. It also helps to be 25 years old and to have been through seven years of rigorous training to prepare for combat. I am sure it makes me a little tougher and perhaps better able to cope mechanically with the danger when it arises. Despite these advantages, one does not go through combat and experience what I have experienced without being affected in some manner. I have come to notice a certain smell in the air when someone is killed on an operation, and I don't know whether it comes from the dead body, from my own perspiration, from other sources, or simply from my mind.

You really ought to see the countryside around here. When Nels gets me a camera, I'll take some color pictures and send you some. The lush green rice paddies, rolling foothills, palm trees, villages, mountains, etc. are really beautiful. Too bad there is a war going on. I really like the country and the job I have as well, in spite of the many frustrations, discouraging moments, and hard work involved.

As rich and beautiful as the scenery may be, the smells leave a little bit to be desired, especially in and around the villages. The smells include a pungent fish sauce (*nuoc mam*), the strong local tobacco (like Turkish cigarettes), burning excrement, and the odors created by animals running loose. I have gotten used to it, however, and may eventually start using *nuoc mam* for aftershave lotion!

1LT Lang is back from the hospital to stay, and seems to be doing pretty well. He stated his appreciation for my help on the day of the shooting and for the American medical treatment during his stay in our hospital in Qui Nhon, so that was nice.

There's been too much media emphasis on excessive force by U.S. troops, and not enough on the truc terrorists who commit virtually all the atrocities—the VC. They routinely assassinate, kidnap, destroy huts, etc. as a matter of policy, just to intimidate the civilians and demonstrate we can't protect them all the time. They killed, without provocation, the parents of one young boy (Tham—pronounced "Tom") from a nearby village; my A team unofficially adopted him and are taking care of (and spoiling) him, and he's a big reason we are building this school nearby. Anyway, U.S. troops may occasionally overreact or mistakenly bomb friendly forces or civilians, but not often or as a matter of policy. The problem is that U.S. TV cameras are often around to show those occasions and broadcast them back home. There are no media present when the VC commit their atrocities. If anything, our forces are unduly reluctant to use force; I've had artillery strikes refused since they would hit what appear on old maps to be villages but in reality are empty, and this gets frustrating.

**FitzGibbon with Tham, an orphan adopted by the
American Special Forces A Team at Ha Tay.**
Daniel H. FitzGibbon

I went to Qui Nhon for a commander's conference last week, my first time out of camp overnight in two months. Didn't get much accomplished, but enjoyed the return to a form of civilization for a change. I did get a little tired of hearing some B team staffers who live in decent quarters with good facilities and plenty of chow complain about how tough life is. I was actually glad to return to camp. Speaking of staffers, I once made some computations and concluded that only about 10 percent of our troops in Vietnam are really combat soldiers, humping the hills on a regular basis, while the other 90 percent are essentially support people who might as well be spending the war in New Jersey for all the danger and deprivations they go through.

Our operations this past week have consisted of one company on a big, extended operation with the 173rd Airborne Brigade south of here, which has so far been a waste of time due in part to the slow pace and heavy support used by the 173rd. The rest of our operations have been oriented toward rice harvest security for farmers and protection for villagers. The VC have stepped up their night actions, kidnappings, and propaganda in the villages to the north of us, and so far I can't get the district people up there to send any Regional Forces/Popular Forces (RF/PF) troops in to protect the people. Obviously, we won't have much credibility with the villagers if we can't even protect them at night when they are only 3 or 4 kilometers from our camp.

My intelligence sergeant, SFC Smith, is home on a reenlistment leave and my senior medic, SGT Daniels, is home on emergency leave for his grandmother's funeral, so I'm a bit shorthanded. I have a 1LT Scotti, a short, feisty, and likeable Italian from New York, assigned now, who is handling the intelligence work and will move up to CA/PO officer when my XO, 1LT

View from Ha Tay looking north.
Daniel H. FitzGibbon

Mundhenk, leaves in June and 1LT Allen moves up to XO. So I'm temporarily fat on officer strength and short five of 11 NCO's. Things should get worse with my team sergeant leaving next month, my XO, engineer, and senior medic leaving in June, and prospects for replacements uncertain.

I have no idea what effect the planned peace negotiations will have on my detachment's stay at Ha Tay, the type of operations we conduct, or my personal status regarding discharge from the army. We have been told to step up offensive saturation operations since Charlie is probably hurting, and to stop referring to search and destroy operations as such, apparently out of respect for Bobby Kennedy's dislike of the term; we now call them saturation patrols, ambush operations, recon patrols, etc., i.e., the same thing with a different name. I don't imagine peace will come quickly, and if de-escalation or withdrawal occurs, the Special Forces camps (first to come in) will undoubtedly be the last to leave (well after our conventional combat units and most of our support personnel leave). Most of the Vietnamese people I've talked to are not very concerned about our withdrawal; many think it will not occur and that President Johnson will actually run again. I expect that, unless Hanoi really balks at negotiations badly or something else happens, we'll start withdrawing combat units this fall, but of course that's only personal speculation. I just hate the idea of pulling out of areas like this to which we've brought a reasonable degree of pacification, security, and development and where Charlie is definitely hurting and living with such difficulty, and of negating the effect of the many lives lost, just to give this all back to Charlie. I have no doubt that our withdrawal to coastal defensive positions or major population centers would result in a wholesale takeover of other areas by VC and eventual strangulation of the isolated areas we do secure. Of course, all this is above my head.

Well, that's about it for now. Am still getting your letters regularly, your packages periodically, and now the papers sporadically, and I appreciate all of it. Nancy sent me a picture of the kids (Darren with wet britches) and I'd like more, also pictures of the wedding.

Take care of yourselves and keep those cards and letters coming in.

Love,
Dan

---

19 May 1968

Dear Folks,

I'm finally sitting down to write after what's been a long delay due mostly to heavy operations. Thanks much for your info on finances, etc., Dad, particularly the good news about the car trade. I took care of the necessary insurance paperwork with no problems. Sounds like you made quite a deal on the car, if the VW is in as good a shape as you indicated. Got a book on "How to Pass the Law School Admissions Test" today—plan to clear the mush and cobwebs out of my head before taking it.

Glad you liked the flowers, Mother. I had specified in my original letter to the florist and reiterated on my order that I wanted the flowers for delivery on the day before Mother's Day, but guess they still didn't get the word. Anyway, I trust you had a happy Mother's Day and also enjoyed the flowers, although I'm sorry they couldn't match up better.

Am having a hard time getting squared away with the 173rd Airborne Brigade regarding their control over my CIDG troops. Since my TAOR is included within theirs, and since my detachment is under their operational control, they feel that they control my troops and can send them wherever they want (even 20 km outside my TAOR) on far-fetched missions of their own choosing. I keep explaining patiently that he may control me and my team but does not control the VNSF nor the 600 man CIDG force—the VNSF controls them. They can't buy that, so I've had several difficult conversations with their commanding general (BG Allen, whom I knew in the U.S. Army Europe). It's nice to be getting out of the army. I'm getting full support from my Special Forces bosses, but BG Allen isn't budging either. They also think that our troops should be as capable of full-time operations as theirs, even though theirs are strictly maneuver battalions (no medical patrols, civic action, camp construction, or similar missions), are here on one-year tours (some of my CIDG have been fighting for 20 years) and are under a disciplinary code (mine are not—not even the VNSF can punish a CIDG soldier for going AWOL, refusing to obey orders, or quitting under fire). As a result, we've had a couple of bad scenes where my CIDG have been assigned ridiculous missions way out of the TAOR, far from their homes and families, and have "quit" on their VNSF leaders. While I can't condone the CIDG quitting by any means, and in fact rushed out with my counterpart to get them going again, I can understand the problem and keep trying to get the 173rd to understand it as well.

My relations with 1LT Lang have improved considerably— a tribute, I think, to tact, patience, and bending on small issues. He's done much more the way I want things done than he ever did for my predecessors, and we've even become sort of friends in a distant manner. I'm still having trouble getting all my A team members to treat the VNSF A team objectively and patiently. I have to climb all over my people when they exercise the luxury of a temper, regardless of the extent of the aggravation, since they detract from the rapport I've been trying to build.

My team has changed a bit since I last mentioned them individually. 1LT Mundhenk is the XO, but will be leaving in about three weeks. 1LT Allen will move from CA/PO officer to XO when he leaves. 1LT Scotti came in about two months ago and will take over as CA/PO officer—he's a hard-charging, positive attitude-type soldier and a real potential asset. MSG Franco, my team sergeant, left on 5 May for the U.S. His temporary replacement is SFC Smith, my former intelligence sergeant. My new intelligence sergeant is named SFC Hayes—a well-experienced SF soldier who really appears to be good. SFC DeLeon is back in camp—he had been here before—he's the one from Guam. I've got him as light weapons (small arms) supervisor, and SFC Grau (my best all-around soldier) as heavy weapons (mortars) supervisor. My commo supervisor, SFC Roese (also a real fine soldier), just got promoted from Staff Sergeant (SSG). He finally has an assistant, SGT Ripple, who just came in from B team and got promoted yesterday from SP4. My senior medic, SGT Daniels, went to the U.S. last month on emergency leave when his grandmother died and will not be coming back since he was scheduled to leave in June anyway. My medic now is SGT Peterson, who was also just promoted from SP4 and who has gained a lot in maturity and effectiveness since I've been here. My engineer is SP5 (equiv. to SGT) Spaulding, who has been great but leaves next month. So I presently have four officers counting myself (one Captain and three 1LTs) and eight NCOs (5 SFCs and 3 SGTs), so I'm over one officer until Mundhenk leaves and under one medic and one engineer.

SFC DeLeon (right), the A team's heavy weapons specialist at Ha Tay, poses with Vietnamese Special Forces Master Sergeant Rao.
Daniel H. FitzGibbon

Action has been hot and heavy here this month—I was in the field 11 of the first 15 days of the month. We killed five VC on one operation, the camp got mortared by NVA, and we killed 130 NVA on another operation. It all started on one operation from 1–5 May, when SFC Grau and I took a company to the west of camp into the Crowsfoot.

Dad, you referred in your letter to the Crowsfoot, and that's the series of stream valleys starting west of camp about 10 km—together, they are shaped like a crow's foot, needless to say. I went into the northern valley. For a good account of the Crowsfoot, the Kim Son River area, the attack on LZ Bird, etc., read *Battles in the Monsoon* by BG S. L. A. Marshall—the book tells about my area and I'm sure was the reference that ex-helicopter pilot had in mind. Also, the An Lao river north of camp about 15–20 km is the area where the 36 Special Forces troops on a special recon mission landed and all but two were killed before a First Cavalry Division thrust into the area. You might be interested in *The New Legion* by MSG (Ret.) Donald Duncan, which describes recons into that area. Both books are critical of field commander actions and Duncan's book is outright anti-USASF propaganda, but nevertheless give you a feel for my TAOR.

Anyway, we moved along the valley floor, stumbled across five local force VC getting water before returning to their caves/bunkers, and managed to kill them all. The rest of the time we spent climbing mountains, learning to appreciate the pain of carrying a heavy rucksack up mountains in 115 degree Fahrenheit temperature with little water available.

When I returned on 5 May, I sent a company-sized operation into the 506 valley SE of camp. At that time, there was a heavy contact east of the 506 in the valley where Highway 1 passes through, where one U.S. company lost about 25 killed but killed 61 NVA.

Vietnamese Special Forces Sergeant Anh (left), "a real fine soldier," and FitzGibbon prepare to move out to the 506 valley to reinforce a besieged company.
Daniel H. FitzGibbon

On 7 May, that company of mine crossed through a clearing with high ground on two sides and coconut palms on the other two. Just then they caught small arms and automatic weapons fire from an entrenched battalion in bunkers on all four sides—one helluva ambush. My people formed a perimeter (SFC Hayes and SGT Peterson were the USASF advisors) by backing up against a rice paddy dike and called in artillery and air strikes. Losing six dead and about 16 wounded, I figured I'd best prepare some reinforcements to move in, so SFC Grau and I gathered up 70 CIDG and we combat assaulted by helicopter into the middle of the perimeter. The CIDG were so demoralized they just sat there stunned—refusing to carry dead to the choppers and to treat wounded. The LLDB just hid, so the USASF had to do it all. The four of us USASF treated wounded, carried them to safety, and rounded up loose weapons from dead and wounded (we were to lose four more dead and 24 more wounded). I also called in air strikes and napalm—all the time we were in the open drawing sporadic small arms, machine gun, and mortar fire. I brought one napalm strike close to my position to silence the worst machine gun and brought a 500 lb. bomb onto the offending mortar. Still the CIDG wouldn't move, so the USASF had to carry the excess carbines, burn the excess ammo and heavy weapons, lead an assault on the coconut palm bunkers to make a breakthrough, and finally the CIDG followed. I took them about 2.5 km up the road (506) where we set up for the night—we got probed two times and one more CIDG was killed that night. I wish I had a dollar for every time I've sat up at night after a probe or attack waiting anxiously for dawn to come; dawn represents a moral and psychological victory. Our Dawn certainly does have a pretty name. The following morning there was a heavy fog that prolonged our uncertainty, but eventually SFC Grau and I returned to camp, mission accomplished, leaving what was left of the original company operation in the 506. We counted 18 NVA killed on our breakthrough, and know we got much more from the bombs and napalm. I was too busy to be scared during the whole thing, but did feel a bit uneasy taking the chopper ride into the middle of the perimeter—I was so helpless sitting on it that I couldn't have done anything if we were shot down, as one chopper already was. I also got a bit weary of seeing and smelling people with half their heads shot off and most of their flesh and muscle ripped up, but such is war. I don't know how I made it OK—I was in the open enough and plenty of people near me were killed or wounded. Luck of the Irish, I guess.

I know napalm has a bad reputation back in the States because it seems too cruel to burn people (although I doubt if it's much worse to be burned than blasted), but it truly saved my life in the 506 valley. The enemy was too close for us to use high explosive bombs or artillery shells, since shell fragments would easily have carried across our position. The virtue of napalm is that it has a very small blasting radius, and we were able to limit its burning force to the position where the enemy was located without endangering our own troops. I have no doubt that, but for napalm, I would not be around today.

That night after returning I was outside the TOC insuring our 4.2 inch mortar was laid in on our company position when I saw flashes of light from 3 km NE of camp. I then saw and felt mortar rounds coming in. So, I just had the 4.2 inch mortar pop rounds out at the flashes, called the artillery to do the same, and contacted a FAC overhead to adjust onto the target. It went so smoothly, and it was so coincidental that the FAC was in the air, that the mortar was being laid with its full crew present and that I happened to be where I could see the flashes, that I'm sure Charlie thinks we're the fastest guns in the West. Needless to say,

Members of Ha Tay's Civilian Irregular Defense Group and FitzGibbon wait to be transported to the 506 valley via helicopters from the camp's runway.
Daniel H. FitzGibbon

Charles got off about 22 rounds and then was completely wiped out. We suffered no damage.

Two days later (10 May), a CIDG Mobile Strike Force (Mike Force) Company from Qui Nhon and a CIDG company from Camp Dong Tre brought in to reinforce us got hit in the 506 near the same place my company got hit. They got pretty battered, and we lost one USASF killed (Tom Swan, a nice young 1LT from North Carolina who commanded the Mike Force), three other USASF wounded, 14 CIDG killed, and another 60 CIDG wounded. I put one company on the bare-topped hill east of the site to block off the NVA withdrawal, and one company on the bare-topped hill to the west to do the same, called in air strikes, maneuvered the two companies up the hill to the west, and brought out two more companies personally from camp. We spent about five days cleaning the place up and, after suffering heavy initial losses before I sent the companies out, we proceeded to kill 130 regular NVA and wound 250 more (the 130 dead are by body count—the 250 wounded by two separate and confirming intelligence reports). So, I came back from that on the 15th, have been getting reorganized since then, and have sent out a couple of platoons and one company to other areas NW and SW of camp to keep Charlie off balance.

I thought the 173rd Airborne was unhelpful, except for helicopter support, during the whole thing. I had to commit my troops since they wouldn't commit theirs, despite my urging, then they ended up chewing out my boss for sending me two Mike Force companies and the one Dong Tre company without using 173rd troops first. Finally, now that everything has died down and Charlie has apparently left the 506, the 173rd just today has brought two battalions into the 506.

After the battles were over, I received a congratulatory telegram from a rear admiral named [Elmo R.] Zumwalt, who claims to be head of U.S. Navy operations inside the country of South Vietnam. Since the navy has virtually nothing going on in the country aside from river patrols in the Delta, this apparently gives Zumwalt plenty of time to do things like send out congratulatory telegrams. Nonetheless, I'm always happy to take a compliment, even from a navy man.

Set up a camp celebration on the 17th—we had a VN entertainment team in from Qui Nhon, called off operations except for two platoons and our regular three observation posts, served extra chow and let the CIDG cool it for a change (much to the chagrin of the 173rd). I thought they deserved it and told them so.

One of the many things which drives me crazy when I read media accounts of our activities here is seeing our CIDG troops referred to as "mercenaries." It is true that we recruit and pay these people to fight, but this is true of most soldiers in most armies. They are fighting to defend their own families and homeland, unlike mercenaries who are recruited in Europe to fight for or against revolutionary forces in Africa. Our soldiers do have a lot more at stake than money in this war, so the mercenary label is both inaccurate and derogatory.

I normally don't keep war souvenirs—I have thrown away or given away weapons, knives, uniforms, hats, helmets, documents, etc., not particularly caring to have things to remind me of the shot-up NVA soldiers, unlike some guys away from the action who revel in junk like that. Nonetheless, I thought you might be interested in some of the NVA propaganda evidenced by these stamps, pamphlet, and leaflet. Obviously, the NVA takes great pleasure in the anti-war demonstrations in the U.S. The one stamp is in reference to Norman Morrison, "Noman Morrixon" according to the NVA, who you will recall self-immolated his way to immortality in front of the Pentagon.

FitzGibbon, "looking dazed in the 506." His counterpart, Lieutenant Lang, is to his right rear wearing the "Walter Brennan hat."
Daniel H. FitzGibbon

Things should stay hot here for some time, and I'm not referring to the temperature alone. Two Special Forces camps elsewhere have been overrun within the last week, and for motivation the NVA has the fact today (the 19th) is Ho Chi Minh's birthday, the peace talks to influence, and the prospective psychological impact of knocking off big fine bases like mine. Tomorrow I continue efforts to fix up my perimeter—we will cut grass around the wire, install trip flares (I have finally received 800 trip flares and 250 more Claymores), lay out tanglefoot (inter-tangled barbed wire placed six inches above the ground), and set up more Claymores. As soon as I get some jelly-like napalm thickener, we can finish my fougasse row. Then I'm going to send a letter to Ho Chi Minh inviting him to try and take this place. I think he'd have a hard time now with all the concrete bunkers we've put up and all the extra fences we've laid.

I plan to go to Pleiku in about four days to brief my C team CO on the 506 action and readjust the property hand receipts for the camp. This will be my second trip out of camp in the three months or so I've been here, so I'm anxious to break out and relax a bit.

Thanks for the wedding pictures—you all looked good and Nancy was quite beautiful. Of course Mother, Dad, and Julie looked real fine, and Dawn was simply precious with her long hair. Doug looked very handsome and grown up in his picture. I would have liked to have seen a picture of Darren and Dana—I'm sure they were equally cute.

Incidentally, I voted in the primary, but don't think my vote arrived in time to be counted. I received my application on 27 April, sent it out the same day, received my ballot on 5 May and sent it out the same day also, so doubt if it arrived on time. Kindly inform the clerk that mail for me sits in Qui Nhon until a chopper comes out to camp and sits here until someone comes to pick it up. If I'm in the field I don't get it until I return. So please tell them to send it real early (application at least one month before the November election) so my vote can count.

Well, that's all for now. Operations and Charlie permitting, I'll try to keep you better informed. Take care of yourselves.

Love,
Dan

---

23 June 1968

Dear Folks,

I see I've missed Julie's birthday, Father's Day, and Mother's birthday (soon), but rest assured I was thinking of each of you on your day as always and hope you enjoyed yourselves. By the way, please don't send me anything for my birthday—I couldn't keep anything decent over here with the heat, dirt, and humidity and don't need anything anyway.

Regarding your questions, Mother, now that the dry season is in full force, the heat gets to about 125–130 degrees Fahrenheit by about 11:00 in the morning—our thermometer just runs to 120 and it reaches that point by 10:00 a.m. It starts at 110 at about 8:00 a.m. and stays above 100 until 7:00 p.m. or so. Nights are usually about 95 degrees. So you can see it's impossible to keep from sweating profusely just sitting inside reading, let alone going on operations. I'm not complaining, just informing you about the weather. My weight is down somewhat—I have no scales so don't know exactly, but I think I'm better off without the excess fat around my sides. I'm sure some people would like to spend a little while over here to lose some weight—we'll call it the "Vietnam Diet." My neck still aches a little from the fall I made off the APC when it flipped into the ditch, particularly when wearing a pack on operations (and I've been on three more since my last letter). When I was in Pleiku about one month ago, I had my neck x-rayed and found I had a compression fracture in one of my vertebrae behind my neck. The doctor said he would have put me in a neck brace had he known about it at first but now says to go on as I have been and gave me some pills to take. I'm not at all worried about it and am keeping up with my usual pace.

While I was waiting to be x-rayed and talk to the orthopedic surgeon, the Dustoff medical evacuation helicopters began to bring in a bunch of Americans wounded when a Fourth Infantry Division convoy was ambushed on the road from Pleiku to Kontum. As I watched the succession of young American soldiers carried in, with arms and legs missing and with massive wounds, I felt embarrassed and petty to think I was there being treated for a minor neck injury. I almost got up and walked out in shame.

While I was in Pleiku, I saw my friend Marty Green, who runs the C team Mobile Strike Force (Mike Force) which is deployed to various hot spots around II Corps. I also visited the local ARVN Hospital, where I had a chance to chat with several of my CIDG troops from Ha Tay, who were recuperating from wounds from prior operations and seemed happy to have company.

I get your letters the following Saturday or Sunday after you write them, occasionally later if we get no chopper or FAC aircraft bringing our mail. They usually arrive at B team on Friday. I get the newspapers from two to three weeks late, and think I have gotten all packages you sent. The packages are fine, particularly the stuff with the toiletries in it (the cookies are delicious), and if you can keep sending about one per month I would appreciate it. Also I have purchased a guitar up at Bong Son—a real good one for only $20, so am staying in practice, learning new chords, and teaching some of my team members how to play. They all say I'm great but maybe that's because I'm the boss. If you can find any good popular or folk books with music, chords, and chord charts that would help a lot.

Things have been going quietly in my TAOR now. Our big fight during May apparently drove two NVA regiments up to the NW to regroup and train replacements. I imagine they will try to come back and hit hard shortly. All we're playing with now are local force VC units—they've mortared us twice more and snipe/harass us quite a bit, have ambushed some vehicles on the road north of camp, and have hit our CIDG village north of camp and the Popular Forces (PF) platoon guarding the bridge north of camp. We've had trouble getting contact with them under favorable circumstances although we're pushing quite a bit—this is one of the reasons I think this war will never end in our favor. Despite our massive buildup and fire superiority, we are really little further along in weeding out local VC infrastructures, destroying and denying base areas and infiltration routes, etc. Every victory we have succeeds in merely temporarily reducing an enemy force and temporarily securing an area—we cannot hit them all. If we punish the major units as we have in the past, and even if we stop all NVA infiltration, we will still have to fight the hard-core local VC who have been at it for years. We killed one VC 1½ months ago who had been hiding in the hills for at least six years by the documentation he had on him. He seems to be more willing to live as he does than we are to fight as we have been. If we destroy the major units, the VC will just revert to a lesser state of insurgency but the movement won't die. I get upset when I think that the people don't care enough to become involved—recently, the VC set up an ambush site for three days only 2–5 km north of camp, killing three Americans when it was sprung, and the people there never bothered to warn us. These are the same people to whom we've provided a new school, refugee support, food, medical care, etc. It's a bit disheartening to find that simple humanitarian efforts, seemingly well directed and incorporated into a psychological operations program, have met little success. Therefore, I predict that Charlie will eventually force us out of the war (through an honorable, negotiated settlement), under terms we feel to be favorable, then continue the war under terroristic form until we return or the VC win. I don't sound too hopeful, do I?

We were all sorry, angry, and disgusted to hear about Bobby Kennedy's assassination. That must be very hard on the Kennedy family.

We just had a recent incident at the "VC village" of Vinh Hoa which left a bad taste in my mouth. I had a small local operation running north of Vinh Hoa that was fired upon by VC who had encamped within Vinh Hoa. My patrol called in for assistance, so several of us took off with a jeep, a few CIDG troops, and one of the Duster vehicles with the 40 mm Gatling guns. We reached the point where our operation was pinned down, so I gave the order to return fire into the village of Vinh Hoa. We did so, but the Duster got carried away and by the time I got them to stop the village was practically leveled. We crossed the river into Vinh Hoa not knowing what to expect. The first thing I saw was a cow sitting calmly chewing its cud, with part of its head blown off and dripping blood profusely. I went a little bit farther and heard a baby crying, and found the baby in good health lying next to his dead mother. A part of my troops under

1LT Allen had gone to the far side of Vinh Hoa to look for VC retreating into the rice paddy and hills beyond. 1LT Allen reported that, while he found no VC (just blood trails), he did find another mother and infant, both of whom were dead. Needless to say, I felt terrible and was quite shaken by the incident. I'm satisfied morally that we had every right to return fire into a village from which VC were attacking and pinning down one of our patrols. I'm also satisfied that the VC were the ones morally responsible for these deaths and this destruction since they were the ones who chose to use this village and these people as their shield. They had to assume that we would not sit there and let them attack us without returning fire. I also realize that this incident pales next to some of the intentional destruction our forces inflicted on civilian populations during WW II, including the fire bombings of Dresden and Tokyo and the atomic bombings of Hiroshima and Nagasaki, each of which killed several hundred thousand people in pursuance of a strategic bombing policy. Still, it was a sad and sickening experience that continues to haunt me.

On a less somber note, one of the problems with my position is being a mere captain with what I consider the responsibilities of a lieutenant colonel. This means that every staff officer with a rank of major or above who comes to inspect some petty area he is responsible for feels he can order me to do whatever he considers appropriate. I got one visit from an Air Force major who chewed me out because our runway did not sufficiently fence off civilians who tended to walk across it with their animals from time to time. The fact that the runway is used only about once a week was irrelevant to his position. He had a decent point, but pedestrians on the runway are not a high priority for me. I think the lesson is that the real enemy is not the communist forces but higher headquarters.

**A 175 mm artillery piece from the American artillery battery located
next to the Ha Tay camp and airstrip.**
Daniel H. FitzGibbon

Speaking of visiting majors, the 175 mm battery next to camp is part of an artillery battalion located about 15 miles away. A major from the staff of that battalion came to see me to tell me that the battery had recently launched a weather balloon that was shot down by one of my CIDG troops, who apparently saw the balloon as an opportunity to indulge in some recreational shooting. He said that the battery was planning to send up another weather balloon that day, and asked if I would kindly have my troops refrain from shooting at it. I said I would, and got the word out to 1LT Lang, who in turn got the word out to all of the CIDG company commanders. A little while later, I watched the weather balloon take off and get about 100 feet in the air when it was shot down by a rifle fired within my camp. You can imagine my dismay and embarrassment when I found out that the culprits were my two lieutenants, Allen and Scotti, whom I had not bothered to warn since I couldn't believe they would do something so stupid and juvenile. The artillery major was livid, 1LT Lang was amused, my sergeants were hysterical, and my lieutenants were badly chastised by me until I eventually found a little humor in the situation. The incident reminded me of two more important lessons. One, never overestimate the intelligence and maturity of your officers, and two, an assumption is the mother of all foul-ups.

While preparing for the LSAT, I have found that my mind has become a bit rusty, particularly regarding reading comprehension. While I've read a lot and mostly best sellers, I have read for enjoyment and not for "intellectual stimulation," so am not used to picking out details or digesting deep thoughts. I doubt if I will do well on general background either, since that is oriented to classical music, art, literature, etc. and I've never been too much on those topics. I still think I'll do well, particularly considering some of the lesser brains who have made it, but probably not well enough for a real good school.

Well, I think I'll close for now. Must get back to work. I'm less worried about getting shot than I am about getting an ulcer, particularly having to tolerate the whims of BG Allen, the 173rd's friendly commanding general.

Take care.

Love,
Dan

---

30 June 1968

Dear Folks,

Just a brief, quick note to let you all know I am well and that nothing much is going on.

As I believe I mentioned last week, all the enemy units in this area have moved north of my TAOR except for small local VC units and a few NVA units scattered out in what appear to be security forces for caches sites, base camps, and political indoctrination classes. Enemy infiltration along prominent routes has continued, but instead of large units moving to battle staging areas the infiltrations are mostly new recruits moving to training areas. I've been trying to concentrate operations on multiple and scattered platoon-sized ventures with a company reaction force on standby, to hunt out the local VC units and block infiltration routes. Thus far, my counterpart has gone along only part way with my ideas. Our contacts have been limited to small engagements, with the VC taking advantage of some brief opportunity, then getting out before our heavy stuff can get in on them. I got into some pretty heavy stuff when I was out on a platoon ambush the other day. We were moving into position when we got hit by a platoon of VC. Bullets zinged by all over the place but none of our people got hit. I called in artillery (8 inch howitzers with a large destructive radius) and air strikes, then moved in to assess. There were only six bodies found, but numerous blood trails.

My current B team boss, Col. Connelly, is going to I Corps (North) to take over the C team and all the A camps up there. I like him a lot and told him to keep me in mind if he has any interesting A camps open. Otherwise, I'm content to remain here for a year, then extend for another tour to do something different.

According to Col. Connelly and Col. Johnson (C team commander at Pleiku), my camp is the best in II Corps (among 20 camps), but maybe that's what they tell all the guys. Anyway, it's all very gratifying, and I think a lot of them as well.

Received a package from Julie and the kids on 26 June—five days after postmark. I don't need anything and didn't want anyone to get me a thing, but appreciate the presents and am looking forward to opening them. Thanks much. Hope Mother and Julie had happy birthdays and Dad a happy Father's Day.

I'm continuing my preparation for the LSAT 3 August, including taking a practice test. I find I'm weak in English grammar, of all things. It seems I've forgotten a few too many rules despite my prior proficiency. If you can get my English grammar book from West Point (or if not available, from high school) and send to me as soon as possible I would greatly appreciate it. I need to spend a couple of weeks reviewing grammar rules. I did very well in math principles and cases and data interpretation, and pretty well in figure classification, but just passing in reading comprehension, grammar, and general background. Hope my preparation will allow me to improve when I take the test for real in August. You might throw in a brief guide to art and music appreciation if you can get one quickly. Unlike most people, I do quite well when cramming, as I can remember many things for a short period of time, but unfortunately fail to retain them after a while. Now, what was I saying?

I hope to be able to get my extension leave OK. Am trying to get my friend Nels to come along (Nels Marin, who is Fifth Special Forces Group adjutant and a good friend from Berlin) and perhaps Bob Mack (has an A camp in III Corps—also a good friend from Berlin).

My counterpart just made captain, or Dai-Uy (Die-wee) in Vietnamese. The CIDG and my own A team call me Dai-Uy, incidentally, at least to my face (no doubt worse when I'm not around!). My code name on the radio is "Sparse Detour Zero-Six." The Sparse Detour part is simply a random combination of two plain words; the zero-six means I'm the commander. My other A team members are Sparse Detours with other numbers geared to their positions.

When it's my turn to perform guard duty at camp, I usually sit in our mess hall and write letters or read books. Occasionally I try to shoot rats using "rice rounds," which are regular shotgun shells that have been cut open to remove the buckshot; I then insert uncooked grains of rice in place of the buckshot and seal with melted candle wax. This way, if I see a rat I can do considerable damage to him without damaging the facilities.

Speaking of pests, this area has the most aggressive, meat-eating red ants I've ever seen. One time on an operation, I came under attack and dove into a hole that, to my dismay, had a number of red ants that started nipping at me. Faced with the choice of possibly getting shot vs. definitely getting bitten, I jumped out of the hole and took my chances on the bullets. Another interesting creature is

FitzGibbon at Ha Tay.
Daniel H. FitzGibbon

the pygmy rattler, a miniature rattlesnake about 18 inches long that, unlike its larger North American cousin, likes to attack even when it is not provoked. One time on an operation we spotted one, and one of the CIDG put a stick on the ground in front of it. We stood around and watched it attack and bite the stick before we did him in for good. There are also leeches around here, especially during the rainy season. The old story about how you can't pull them off and have to burn them off with a lighted cigarette is absolutely accurate. I knew my cigarette smoking would come in handy one of these days. I also saw a tarantula sitting on a log one time, and almost sat down on it before one of my troops spotted it.

Well, I hope you are all well. I'll keep in touch and let you know what's going on.

Love,
Dan

---

12 September 1968

Dear Folks,

Am sitting up pulling a three hour guard shift (3:00 a.m. to 6:00 a.m.) back at camp after two weeks away for R & R and miscellaneous stuff at different HQs.

Tokyo was great—very clean, bustling, and modern and there was much to do. It was really nice to see green grass, paved highways, and nice gardens for a change. We (Nels Marin and I) left Cam Ranh Bay on 2 September, catching a C-130 to Tachikawa Air Force Base, and from there went by train to Tokyo. We stayed in a nice hotel for five days for $5 per day, but that was the only cheap thing there. We spent most of our time checking out Tokyo and visiting all the sights there—not being anxious to rush up and down all Japan trying to see so much but being more intent on having a good time and relaxing. We left early 8 Sept. by C-141 (Jet) and got back to Saigon at about 1600. I stayed the night in Saigon at the Special Forces liaison detachment there and returned the next day.

The movie "The Green Berets" was recently completed and copies were rushed to all camps in Vietnam for special screenings. I enjoyed the movie, as I happen to believe in most of the story being told, but the combat scenes themselves were very unrealistic and laughable. The CIDG troops got a big kick out of that part of it.

A few days ago a Duster being improperly towed ran over one of my CIDG who was riding a bike nearby, and squashed him grotesquely under a track. A Duster is supposed to be towed by two cables, one from a hook on each side of the front, so that it will move in a generally straight line forward. In this case, the Duster was being towed by one cable attached to a hook on only one side of the front, apparently because someone chose to save a little time. As a result, the Duster moved erratically when towed and ran over my soldier. Since the incident occurred within my area of responsibility, I gave a report to the B team and it was relayed to the Duster battery commander. It turns out that the lieutenant in charge of the Duster squad next to my camp, in his report, stated that the Duster was being properly towed and that my soldier simply rode his bicycle in front of it. The lieutenant's commanding officer came to see me for confirmation of my report, which I gave him, at which time he relieved the lieutenant of his command on the spot and sent him back to base.

Activity here has been light as far as major NVA units are concerned but heavy as far as local VC units go. Nearly every day at least one of our operations gets in contact with a small force, but only occasionally is Charlie stupid enough to hang around after doing his damage and wait for our units and artillery to come in. We've received reports the enemy is moving back into this area in large numbers, so I wouldn't be surprised if we don't get some big action again in a month or two. The monsoons start here in about a month, and that is ideal guerrilla weather. I've been out on a couple more operations since I last wrote but my contacts have been small. I did get mortared again and one round landed within 10 feet of me, but it was a dud. I'm living right, I guess. The picture of the scene when the dud mortar round hit is indelibly frozen in my mind. As we are supposed to do when mortar or artillery is trained on our position, we took off running across a rice paddy into a tree line. While we were running, I heard the "shloop" of the dud mortar round hitting the mud, and looked up to see SFC Grau looking back in my eyes. I can still see him staring at me, the troops in front of him running toward the tree line and the green trees and blue sky in the background, and the picture seems etched in my mind forever.

Sorry about the misunderstanding on the camp getting hit. About 8–10 camps did get attacked (the main one being at Duc Lap about 150 miles SW), and Ha Thanh (north of me with a similar name) had one of its outposts overrun. You don't need to worry or check with the Red Cross like that, since you would surely be notified if anything did happen.

I received a visit a while back from the Deputy Commander of the Fifth Special Forces Group, who wasn't too pleased with me or my operation. His first objection was that I needed a haircut, and things went downhill from there. I guess I should be grateful to him for reinforcing the wisdom of my decision to get out of the army. In any event, in response to his visit, the Command Readiness Team recently created by Group to inspect and evaluate lower unit operations promptly paid us a visit, presumably expected to find fault. It turned out that this team, which was headed up by Captains Mike Shaver and Lee Yarborough, both of whom I know, was very impressed with our operation and gave us a glowing report on their return to Group. The Deputy Group Commander was reportedly astonished and dismayed at their report, but in fairness to him I should mention that I got a haircut before the team visited. In any case, we have been rated the top A team in II Corps so far and a model for the other CIDG camps. I have to give Shaver and Yarborough a lot of credit for their courage in stating the facts as they saw them, notwithstanding how easy it would have been to ingratiate themselves with the Deputy Commander by confirming his opinions. Shaver is a fellow West Pointer who is in for a career, and Yarborough is the son of the general credited with founding the modern-day Special Forces.

Have been getting a lot of visitors lately—we have a new Fifth Special Forces Group commander and he has reportedly thus far kicked out 2 C team commanders, 4 B team commanders, and 8–10 A team commanders, including one entire A team. We've been getting along very well, having just passed the Command Readiness inspection in good shape and having been highly complimented by the Group CO on his last visit, so I am not too worried, but I use this threat as an excuse to push Captain Lang. He has been working pretty hard lately and we have been getting along fairly well. I don't know how much longer I will be here— one normally lasts only 3–4 months and I've been here 7½ so I expect to be moved to a staff job in a few months. I still plan on extending for another tour in VN after I write the Pentagon to insure this won't hurt my chances of getting out of the army. This will mean I will be leaving here around the lst of February for 30 days leave and returning for my second tour. I still plan on taking R & R to Australia in November or December, since this last trip was a leave and I am authorized a seven day leave and a seven day R & R per tour of duty over here.

The A team is continuing to get periodic replacements. My new CA/PO officer, replacing Frank Scotti who was reassigned to the B team, is Jim Wilson, who attended Special Forces school with me. My biggest memory of him from Ft. Bragg was when we were on a field operation and he spotted a huge rattlesnake, which he proceeded to bash to death with an empty ammo can. Obviously a "keeper" who will come in handy here. My new team sergeant, replacing SFC Smith, is MSG Hoskinson, a slightly heavyset, intelligent, articulate, and low-key individual who is likely to be more flexible and better liked by the team members than MSG Franco was. MSG Hoskinson is also Jewish, a fact that adds to the ethnic melting pot represented in the team.

Was surprised to hear about Julie's operation but was very happy to find out all went well. Was also very happy to get her letter—haven't heard from her in a long time. I hope she is feeling better and will be completely well soon.

Was also happy to get letters from Dawn and Dad. Dawn's letter was very well written and enjoyable to read—I sent her a postcard from Japan which you may not yet have received since I sent it through Japanese mail.

I received a letter from Nancy the other day asking me to explain how I can justify fighting in a war when Don, as a conscientious objector, thinks it is immoral to do so. This is a classic philosophical question which no one can answer very well, and I know Nancy felt in the middle between the two viewpoints. I said that I believe that if some people are trying to destroy the freedoms and take the lives of other people, that we have a right and responsibility to step in and protect these lives and freedom and, if necessary, kill the attackers. Otherwise, we would all be at the mercy of the aggressors. I also pointed out, and I hope she took this the right way, that while I am pleased that our country recognizes conscientious objectors and allows them to avoid military service, I think this is a luxury that we as a nation can afford only so long as the number of conscientious objectors is small enough. If we were a nation of conscientious objectors who refused to bear arms to preserve the freedoms and lives of our families, we would soon lose our liberty. Anyway, I don't know if I persuaded her but that wasn't my goal; sometimes you have to rethink your own rationale for doing things and her question gave me the opportunity.

I got the results of my LSAT back and was completely shocked. Test scores run from 200 to 800 with an average score around 500 for the morning phase (like the college boards). My score was 723, which places me in the upper 1 percent of all applicants. The afternoon test was divided into writing and general background, each of which had possible scores from 20 to 80 with a median of 50. My writing score was 76, which puts me in the top 0.5 percent and my general background was a surprisingly high 58 (top 16 percent) which was much better than I thought I would do on art, music, literature, etc. Since the most important scores from an aptitude point of view are the morning phase and the writing phase and since my scores are better than over 99 percent of all persons taking the test in this and previous years, I should be able to get into any law school I want, particularly if they consider my circumstances (VN) and time out of school (four years) when evaluating my score. So how about digging out all my application forms (Harvard, Yale, Michigan, IU, Stanford, Hastings, and Texas) and sending them to me. I will then complete and send in to the schools. Needless to say, the results of that test were most encouraging and surprising.

Dad, I didn't get the cards from Orphie Bridges in time to take to Tokyo so I did not look up any of the people there. I had a hard enough time moving around and communicating (strange language and all writing was done in characters so was not readable) that I probably could not have made it anyway. Besides, as you've probably noticed, when I go on leave I tend to avoid people, obligations, and occasions that require social niceties.

I finally got a camera, a half-frame Olympus Pen FT that I had to order through the PX for $85. Its normal price I believe is at least $25–40 higher in the states. I am still experimenting with it so don't expect any good pictures for a while. I put a roll of color slide film in it in Tokyo (after getting it fixed since the shutter would not work properly) and took only 7–8 shots there. I plan on taking a lot of pictures of the camp and area before the rainy season sets in, so I hope they come out OK.

I got Skip's wedding invitation and would appreciate it if you could send him a gift for me. Have you met his bride yet? This leaves me one of the few bachelors remaining from my high school class but of course I couldn't care less about that.

Well, I'm back in the routine again, fighting my counterpart, the 173rd, my B team, C team, Fifth Special Forces Group HQ, and occasionally even the VC.

Would appreciate it if someone would see the county clerk and tell him that I will need a ballot ASAP. I will send in the application, but if they process it like they did for the primary I won't get it in time for my vote to count. Mail takes at least a week to get to my B team, occasionally three to four days more to get out here (depending on whether a chopper is available) and possibly a couple more days for me to get if I am in the field. To be safe, the clerk should mail the ballot to me a month early to permit the round-trip in time if this is possible. I am totally unenthused about either ticket this year, but have to do my civic duty.

Well, must close and get back to work. Please keep the letters coming.

Love,
Dan

---

3 October 1968

Dear Folks,

Trust you got my last letter OK and know the situation with me. I was informed by my B team CO that the Red Cross sent another telegram inquiring about me, about a week or so after the first one, and after you got my postcard from Japan. I don't know what prompted the second one but hope you are not getting harassing telephone calls or anything like that. Were something to happen to me you would be notified in person by an army officer between 6:00 a.m. and 10:00 p.m., so please ignore anything else.

My last month has seen a step-up of activity and contacts with enemy forces over preceding months, even though the NVA are staying out of this area. We killed 41 VC during September, while losing only one CIDG, and captured four prisoners. I set up one operation about 12 miles SW of camp and went myself with a company. We surrounded a VC way station (small detachment of 15–20 local force VC who provide food, lodging, medical attention, supplies, and guides for transient NVA units), opened fire, and killed 15 VC and captured one without any friendly casualties. We looked like the St. Valentine's Day massacre, but since all were VC and all were armed I have no qualms if their security is bad. Two other operations did about the same, killing six at one time and killing 10, capturing three others. Our more aggressive tactics are paying off, and if we can continue to knock out these way stations we can seriously hamper VC/NVA infiltration through this area. I've always held that elimination of these local force VC, who have been in the villages or mountains for years and who will continue to be long after we leave, is more important in terms of quality than ten times the number of NVA killed.

Actually, the success of this operation was as much due to blind luck as to sound tactics. The operation was run as a joint operation with the Vinh Thanh Special Forces camp located about 30 miles southwest of us. The idea was to drop two companies from each camp at a landing zone (LZ) halfway between the camps, an area virtually untouched by previous operations, and have them walk back to their respective camps with each company taking a different route back. I went out with the 173rd Airborne Brigade helicopter pilot commander the day before the drop to pick the LZ, and selected one site, which was a small clearing among miles and miles of thickly vegetated hills and other small clearings. On the day of the operation, I went in with the first helicopter for the landing, at which time I realized that the LZ I had selected on the ground was not the LZ I had identified on the map, with the result that we were about two miles closer to Vinh Thanh and farther from Ha Tay than I expected. I was still kicking myself for this navigational error as the company I was with began the long march back along a ridgeline when we heard the sound of wood chopping in a valley below. SGT Binh (VNSF) and I gathered the troops and we moved down into the valley through the thick vegetation as quietly as we could, where we spied a VC way station with an undetermined number of North Vietnamese troops present. We were well out of radio contact with any potential assistance, and did not know whether this was an isolated group or part of a regimental size operation known to occupy this general area. Nonetheless, we formed an "L" around the group and, at SGT Binh's signal, opened fire on them. The thing was over in about 45 seconds, by which time we had seized our prisoner, counted the enemy dead, taken whatever documents we could, and headed off for home as quickly as possible. It took another day of marching before we could get into radio contact and arrange for a helicopter to pick up our prisoner. It then took another five days for us to make it back to camp, at which time I got to explain with a red face how this great military victory was due to my navigational error.

I have just received another distinct honor, albeit a dubious one at that. As you know, Duc Lap (Special Forces camp on the Cambodian border) was attacked by two NVA regiments in August and almost overrun. Although the camp held, many deficiencies were discovered and much of the camp was destroyed. As a result, many new policies need to be established, new procedures instituted, and new facilities constructed. Furthermore, the camp is still surrounded by 2½ regiments, receives daily mortar attacks (Ha Tay, incidentally, received two mortar attacks in the past two weeks—one last night), and has problems with the VNSF as well. Anyway, as you've probably guessed, I have been reassigned to Duc Lap to take over as commander and will leave Ha Tay on Sunday 6 October. Since this is a tough position, since Col. Aaron, the Fifth Special Forces Group commander, reportedly chose me over the other A team commanders and other captains, and since Ha Tay's record is so good now, I suppose that this is an honor. At least I've been told that by the C team commander who flew out here today to inform me. One sad, although of course pleasing, aspect is facing the many friends I have gathered, Vietnamese and American, and having to say goodbye to them. Even Captain Lang, who had engaged in continuous fights with my predecessors, begged the C Team commander to get the Fifth Special Forces Group commander to change his mind. Anyway, off I go to another camp and I hope things go as well there as here. We've built a lot of new things, have got a real solid camp and our operations record has been quite outstanding, so I'm rather proud of our accomplishments.

Well, that's about it for now. I doubt if I'll have much time to write in the future but will try to send a note to give you my new address. I think the Detachment is A-239, but I don't know the APO. All my mail will go through the B team at Ban Me Thuot.

Take care of yourselves and keep writing.

Love,
Dan

---

26 October 1968

Dear Folks,

As I indicated in my last letter, I am now at Duc Lap as A team commander after bidding farewell to Ha Tay. I didn't realize at the time how far we had progressed at Ha Tay and how well I had it, but I do now.

My transfer was necessitated because the Duc Lap camp was in such a dismal state—completely destroyed during the attack on 23 August, morale low (280 CIDG assigned out of 640 authorized—half had deserted), training nonexistent, ammo and weapons lying around loose and corroded, and the American detachment was pretty battered as well. I am the third CO in less than a month, so apparently the powers that be consider me either a "miracle worker" or more grist for the mill.

Things are every bit as bad as they sound, and much worse. The camp defense system is poorly organized, communications between alert positions nonexistent, no one knows what to do if attacked, and operations are at a standstill. Files are nonexistent, equipment and supplies are scattered throughout the area, and funds appear to have been neglected or misused. I have organized everybody and assigned tasks and priorities. I'm trying to reorganize the camp defense plan and mortar concentrations, relocate offices and alert positions, and establish adequate alert plans and communications. Things are starting to look better, construction is proceeding adequately, and some improvement in morale is evident. What a job, particularly after having gone the same route to a lesser degree at Ha Tay for eight months and looking forward to a soft staff job.

The NVA has pulled out of the area. Gen. [Creighton W.] Abrams thinks they've quit but I doubt it. Their biggest base in Cambodia (Nam Lyr) is located just inside the Cambodian border only eight miles from my camp. I can see the mountain range easily from here. About two divisions are there now, and they could send tanks or move on foot to my camp in one evening. We can't bomb or patrol in Cambodia, so they are quite secure there. As you can imagine, I could care less if the bombing stops in North VN since it would hardly affect me.

Duc Lap has a 3,500 ft. concrete runway, with the carcass of a crashed C-123 sitting off to one side. Next to the runway is a huge Michelin rubber plantation run by a Frenchman, who allowed the NVA attackers to use it as a staging area for their assault without warning the camp. Needless to say, I'm not a big fan of Michelin right now, though in fairness to the Frenchman I suppose he felt caught in the middle and had to work out some accommodation for his own survival.

I've put in for my second tour of duty, hoping to be assigned to Fifth Special Forces Group HQ in Nha Trang. I should be leaving here on/about 4 February for 30 days leave, where I think I'll spend about a week each in the Philippines and Hawaii settling down en route home. Am still looking for R & R to Australia in December or January.

Dad, how about transferring about $500 from savings into my checking account? I will need to write some checks for application processing and for R & R when it comes. I got your applications and financial statement OK, but several schools were missing. I'll write them again for forms. This is quite a headache trying to apply for seven different law schools, ask for letters of recommendation, take the LSAT, etc. all during a war.

My Olympus Pen F takes outstanding pictures—I took a couple of rolls at Ha Tay and they came out really well. The slides are half frame—35 mm film with ASA from 25 on up is fine if you care to send any. Would appreciate Kodachrome if you can.

Forgot to tell you that Tham, my young friend at Ha Tay, really enjoyed the presents the kids gave him and asked me to relay his thanks. He would ask periodically to see my pictures of all of you and seemed fascinated by your looks, clothes, and surroundings. He's a real fine boy—I've got him in my school at Ha Tay but he keeps playing hooky since he's so far advanced for his contemporaries.

Am trying to work an arrangement with the Fifth Special Forces Group Catholic chaplain to enroll him in a nice orphanage and school in Nha Trang or Saigon. I think it's best for him.

Here in the Central Highlands there is higher elevation, so the weather is cooler and often foggier than in the Ha Tay area nearer the coast. The terrain is more rolling, with less pronounced peaks. The vegetation is very dense, with few rice paddies and other open areas.

The other day some Fourth Infantry Division helicopter gunships spotted one of my local security patrols near camp and opened fire on them, killing two and wounding five. We had notified them that this was an area where we send patrols, and they were supposed to check with us before firing away. A real shame, especially with all the other morale problems here.

I guess that's about it for now. I'll write when I can but chances are few. Keep writing, especially you slow ones who write only once a year. Congratulations to Doug and Dawn for getting into Cub Scouts and Brownies and I hope you enjoy it.

Lots of love,
Dan

---

14 November 1968

Dear Folks,

Am almost completed with preparation and submission of applications for law schools. As you can imagine, getting addresses of personnel for letters of recommendation, writing to these people, getting transcripts, writing checks, filling out applications and scholarship requests, and trying to keep track of all this for seven different schools is quite a pain in the neck, particularly here in Vietnam with nothing available and where so much else has to be done. I'm just about through, leaving me to wait on letters of recommendation, answers from schools, and for the army to let me out of service. I got a letter from the army in response to a question I asked them regarding my second tour, and they indicated that since I will have less than 90 days remaining until my 3 Dec. 69 termination date when I complete my second tour in September, and since part of that 90 days will be leave time, they might let me out in September so I can start law school then. I have noted on all my applications that, even though I may not get out of service in time and may have to request a deferral if accepted, I would like to be considered for the Sept. 69 entering class. Michigan is the only school where the term starts in August, so I have just applied for the fall 1970 term there.

I recently saw an article from the *New York Times* reporting that a psychiatrist had completed a study indicating that the life expectancy of an A team captain in Vietnam, at least in the camps he studied, is only three months. This was reassuring, as I now approach the 10 month mark. He said that one reason for the low survival rate is the effort by the captain to impress his team members by example and by taking extraordinary risks to earn their respect. This could well be the case, as I find myself assigning more operations, and more hazardous operations, to myself than anyone else on the team. It seems to me, though, that the worst part of being an A team leader is the loneliness, the knowledge that you are in charge and ultimately responsible, that there is no one within many miles of your camp to help you out if an emergency arises, and that there are hundreds of people looking to you for their safety and well-being day after day, night after night. After a while it wears on you, and eats away at your stomach. Thank goodness for Tums!

Am getting along well here—much is getting accomplished and so far all of my bosses seem pleased. Still have to face all of the reconstruction and reorganization as purely American projects, since I can't get much support from my counterpart. Sanitation and hygiene continue to be a major problem. I asked for a U.S. Army doctor from Ban Me Thuot to help us with this problem, so he visited, interviewed us to find out everything that was wrong, and wrote a report listing all of our deficiencies. I then got an order directing me to remedy all of the deficiencies. Thanks a lot, Doc! Once again, higher headquarters to the rescue.

The C Team commander at Pleiku wants to pull me up to be his S-3 (operations and training officer), but I would prefer to stay here until I leave, then go to Nha Trang on my second tour.

That's all for now.

Love,
Dan

---

15 December 1968

Dear Folks,

Well, I have another surprise for you. Due to a weird set of circumstances falling into place in my behalf, I am now the area specialist officer in the S-3 section of Fifth Special Forces Group HQ in Nha Trang.

When I submitted my extension for a second tour, my B team, C team, and Group HQ all said they wanted me for their staffs. I wasn't interested in the B team, but the CO of the C team at Pleiku wanted me to go there to be his S-3 (operations and training officer—a major's position). Although this was an interesting offer, I told him no, since I would rather complete the job at Duc Lap until my extension took place and then go to Nha Trang. Meanwhile, Group HQ was pushing to get me to be area specialist officer in Nha Trang, since the incumbent was departing shortly. They sent a major to Pleiku to fill the S-3 position, hoping to satisfy the C team commander, then told him they wanted me in Nha Trang immediately. He then countered by saying that he needed me desperately at Duc Lap and would not release me, even though he had been willing to pull me up from Duc Lap to be his S-3. He then told Col. Aaron, the Group CO, that he needed to keep me, so Col. Aaron (not knowing he had wanted me in Pleiku) told him I would stay at Duc Lap. Meanwhile, the adjutant at Group HQ had cut orders reassigning me to Nha Trang, and the message came to me while I was out in the field and told me to pack my bags for Nha Trang. So I came in to Nha Trang, not knowing that an agreement between Col. Aaron and the C team commander had been made to keep me at Duc Lap. When Col. Aaron saw me here, he asked me what I was doing here; when I told him, he said that if the C team commander was too stupid to notify me to stay, he would keep me in Nha Trang. Anyway, it's nice to feel wanted.

So, here I am in Nha Trang—fairly safe and free of pressure (we have been mortared twice since I got here but this is comparatively peaceful). As area specialist officer, I am supposed to become the Fifth Special Forces Group expert on all A camps, B and C teams, and separate detachments. All reports from the field come in to me. My four NCOs (I have one per Corps area) brief the Group CO each day on operational statistics and enemy contacts, and maintain camp defense folders and information on each camp. I handle all operational reports, including operation summaries and statistics (which are voluminous in this HQ). I am the group operations statistician and also the group briefer. I brief all VIPs who come to Fifth Special Forces Group HQ. This is an interesting job, and I think I'll learn quite a bit about all the camps and the big picture now.

I hated to leave Duc Lap in many respects, but the pressure, work, and constant responsibility were getting old. Now I'm one of those rear-echelon types I always complained about. Here I live in a nice big room with maids, laundry service, boot shining service, and nearby showers and latrines in sparkling condition. Hours are much better, and I have no field duty, although I hope to get out to some of the A camps soon. In my compound we have a PX, movie theater, beautiful officer's club, tailor, and even a Dairy Queen. So life is much better than before, although you would be surprised how many people still manage to complain with all this.

I have received your Christmas package and tree, and thanks very much. I've also received all of your packages with food and toiletries and really appreciate them. Since I am near a PX and have so much money, there is no need for you to ship anything else. Besides, I've accumulated quite a stockpile. Anyway, thanks a million for all of your efforts and time in preparing and mailing me these things—it was almost impossible to get any of this stuff while at an A camp.

Martha Raye's in VN again, traveling around to a bunch of the A camps. She spends a month or two in VN and stays with Special Forces. She stays at the A camps, even overnight, plays cards, and tells jokes like one of the boys. She spent a night out at Ha Tay, I am told, and really enjoyed herself. She also lost about $300 to the team in poker. I haven't seen her yet, as she never made it out to Duc Lap, but I may see her here in a while. She's quite a Special Forces favorite and deserves a lot of admiration.

Tell Dawn that I got her second letter and appreciate it very much. I enjoyed hearing about her Brownie Scouts and her swimming. She writes very well and spells words quite well. I am very proud of you, Dawn.

I don't know whether I told you or not, but when a Catholic chaplain visited Ha Tay I told him about Tham, introduced them and they talked quite a while. The chaplain was quite impressed, so I asked him to see if he could get him into an orphanage some place. None of the team could spend enough time with him, and his education was being stymied at the little school we built. The chaplain said he'd try, and was able to get him into an orphanage in Nha Trang. The team had him all psyched up about going and he was real excited about it. Needless to say, I am going to have to stop over and see him quite a bit while I am here.

Am still planning to go to Australia 2–9 January and then home in February. I may go to Europe and Africa (including Algeria to see Nancy, of course), but I may not be able to get out of here on schedule with all of the big projects coming up in the middle of February. So I'll be home when I make it.

Well, I trust you're all getting ready for Christmas. Hope you have an exciting time, and stay away from the Hong Kong flu.

Love,
Dan

10 January 1969

Dear Folks,

Merry Christmas and Happy New Year. Hope all of you had a fine holiday season and are successfully avoiding the Hong Kong flu.

Thanks so much for the many fine presents. All were very nice and practical as well, and I know I will have great fun with the Scrabble game and everything else.

I took most of the candy and of course your present to the orphanage to see Tham and he was quite delighted to see me again. I went with 1LT Allen, who was with me at Ha Tay and who wanted to see him also. He was real excited about his clothes and insisted on trying them on. All fit perfectly—I am amazed at how well you guessed his sizes.

Christmas was quite nice here—complete turkey dinner and all. Compares favorably to Thanksgiving, which was spent in the field near Duc Lap in a cold rain, with some C Rations and rice.

Just got back from a week in Australia with Nels Marin. We spent the whole time in Sydney, since we just felt like lounging around the beach and hotel. We saw most of the city and went out to an island where the city zoo is located, but did not make it into the backcountry to any ranches. It would have been nice to have spent a couple of days at a big sheep ranch with kangaroos and all but, even though these tours were free and there were many families volunteering to put up soldiers for a couple of days, Nels and I turned it down since it would have meant we would have to be sociable for a couple of days. The weather was beautiful (like July—up to 109 one day), the ocean breeze was nice, and the people were quite friendly. The whole place was easy going, and more like the U.S. than what I picture Britain to be.

Fifth Special Forces Group headquarters got a big lift recently when word reached us that Nick Rowe, a 1960 West Point graduate, who had been captured in the Delta while on a Special Forces operation in 1965, had escaped from VC captivity and found his way to friendly forces.

Still don't know when I'll be home or for how long, but I'll keep you posted. I'll probably call you from Chicago.

Now that I have applied to all these law schools, I wonder what I'll do if all accept me, which would be a nice problem to have. Although I have my priorities in mind, I will probably not be notified in that order and will be given only a short time to accept or reject each admission. I guess I'll play that game when the time comes.

Well, hope all is well. I received many nice cards and even some goodies from many people, even some strangers, over Christmas, so it's nice to know many people at home are thinking about us and supporting our efforts.

Take care of yourselves.

Love,
Dan

---

29 January 1969

Dear Folks,

Just a quick note to let you know all is well and that I should be home by the time you receive this note, or at least shortly thereafter. I am going to Saigon to pick up a passport and should be back in

Nha Trang shortly prior to my departure. I leave from Cam Ranh on the lst of February, and will arrive home a few days after that.

Nels and I have not yet decided how long we will cool it on the West Coast prior to coming on home, but I doubt if it will be too long. We still plan to go to Israel, if everything works out OK with the passport and if we can get visas in there. Beyond that, it will probably be Lisbon, Athens, and who knows where else. I'm not too confident we will be able to get down to see Nancy—I don't expect to have much time, particularly to spend catching trains, buses, and camels to get out to her place, although I am sure she could use a familiar face. We'll just have to see about this.

I know I sound like those rear-echelon types I've ridiculed before, but I have been working my fat rear end off here—plenty of pressure and long hours, but unfortunately, like the army every-where, nearly all of it is self-generated and does not contribute to the success of the war effort. I was happier in many ways out at my camps, even though the food, living conditions, conveniences, and lack of full-time responsibility are somewhat improved (more than somewhat). I've managed to recover from the skin and bones appearance I possessed out at Ha Tay and Duc Lap—I've got a nice roll around my belly now. Perhaps I can do some exercising on my second tour.

I still have heard nothing from any of my law school applica-tions, although I know it's still quite early. I hope I don't get a response with a two week reply deadline while I am on leave.

Well, must close for now. Don't expect me to arrive any certain day, since I have no idea myself. I'll call you from Chicago or Indianapolis to let you know when to pick me up at Indianapolis.

Lots of Love,
Dan

20 April 1969

Dear Folks,

I imagine you're beginning to wonder what's happened to me since I left home on 17 February. Actually, things have been going smoothly and rather uneventfully and there really hasn't been too much to describe.

My postcards kept you fairly well abreast of my travels and I'm afraid that detailed impressions, actions, and reactions would be too lengthy to enumerate. In summary, I didn't care much for Greece (at least what I saw was dirty and I thought we got over-charged too much), found Israel interesting and liked the way they treated foreigners (no great effort to impress, please, or serve—just natural, self-assured and independent), and thought Bangkok was great fun—prettiest women in the world.

Since I've returned, I've been bogged down with my usual recurring reports, briefings, statistics, etc., but find it interesting in spite of the work. I've briefed Gen. Abrams, Gen. [Andrew J.] Goodpaster, and numerous other generals and admirals (nine the past week) and enjoy that, although the briefings make it hard to do my regular job. I enjoy giving briefings and writing them, because I really believe in the Special Forces program and think we're the most effective counterinsurgency force in this country. I might add that so far everyone, from Gen. Abrams on down, claims to have been impressed with my briefings and Col. Aaron, the Group CO, has been very supportive.

I've gotten acceptances from all law schools, and have decided on Harvard after discussing the subject with a couple of Judge Advocate General lawyers here and my friend Roger Parkinson, a Harvard MBA. They all favor Harvard over Yale, in part because Cambridge beats New Haven by far. I know it's more expensive than the other schools, and I don't expect to receive any financial aid, but how can you turn down the best?

Was happy to hear about Tracy and hope Sally is well. She really looked good when Nels and I saw her in New York, and we had a swell though short visit with them. Hope you are passing on my love to Nancy and Sally as I haven't written them lately and will probably have a hard time getting around to it. Assume everyone at home is OK and doing well.

I resubmitted my resignation recently and it just left here for Saigon and Washington. Also sent an advance letter to Department of Army at the Pentagon to get an idea where I stand. Col. Aaron and all claimed to have been reluctant to pass it on but did so with fine endorsements.

Hope to leave here in late August if all goes well.

I may be able to take off on leave the first week in May—don't know where yet but possibly Manila. Will let you know before or by postcard when I arrive.

Well, that's about it. Hope you had a happy 59th, Dad, on 16 March. I was thinking about you on your day.

Lots of love,
Dan

---

10 July 1969

Dear Folks:

Just received Julie's pecan pie and, considering the long trip, it made it in fine style. It was a little runny, but tasted great. I had a couple of pieces and passed it around, since the abundance of bugs and rats here precludes leftovers. No one has yet been able to provide any definite links between the pie and a recent outbreak of ptomaine poisoning, although I have been asked to add a warning on future packages that eating runny pecan pies may be hazardous to your health. Seriously, beautiful, thanks a million for your thought and I did enjoy the pie, although I hope to sample the real thing when I return.

Have still received no official word on my release from service—am beginning to get concerned. If I don't receive anything definite in another five days, will write the Department of the Army again for info. I've started getting my teeth fixed and will get a physical later this month to expedite my departure when I return to the States. I got four fillings yesterday and will get as many next week on the other side (the dental work has nothing to do with Julie's pecan pie!).

Got the application for housing from Harvard and returned it the same day, although my late receipt of it may keep it from reaching Harvard in time. I can't believe that an expensive school like that has living accommodations for only 475 of 1,700 students. I checked all possibilities to increase my chances, with priorities in the low-priced, single room category. Their notice about no parking for first-year students seems to rule out a car. It may be just to discourage cars, but if it isn't and I have to pay $10 to $25 per month for off-street overnight parking I will be hurting. I don't expect to really need a car while I'm there, since I plan to lead a rather monastic life, but I will need a car to get to Harvard since I will have a lot of junk to take along. So if you don't mind, I think my best bet will be to sell the VW. I have already paid for the car insurance, but will be able to get a refund with no sweat. If you want to keep it and continue paying the insurance and property taxes, you are welcome to do so. I consider the car more yours than mine anyway, and it won't be worth much for sale.

Felt real bad about Uncle Larry. He had suffered so much and led such a discouraging existence for so long. I had mailed him a postcard from Taiwan on 24 May, but was obviously too late.

Got a letter from Nancy—didn't say much except that she would be going to Europe on 31 July for vacation so should have a good time. She seems to be adjusting all right now, although I know it's been tough for her.

I appreciated the pictures of Tracy and Sean, and am glad all are doing well. It was good you could get out to see them, and sounds like you had a good time. We had such a good visit when Nels and I were leaving for Europe.

Also got a letter from Max Andress, informing me we would have a reunion of the football team on 5 Sept. (with a visit to a game and introductions at halftime) and a picnic the next day in the country. Sent him a letter with my regrets since I will be registering at Harvard on 5 Sept. Incidentally, if you have an extra picture of me in my beret, I would like for you to pass it on to Max. He wanted a recent picture and that is probably the best I have.

Am scheduled to go to Hong Kong on 5 August for R and R, and expect to spend a bundle on clothes and junk. If there is anything you would like, such as clothes, material, electronics equipment, etc., let me know before I go and I will be glad to get it for you and send it to you. I would like to get you something, so let me know what you want. Nels and I will be going together again.

My time is passing as usual—giving many VIP briefings, preparing numerous operational reports, charts and statistics, collecting all operational reports from the subordinate camps and Mobile Strike Force (Mike Force) units, etc. Also preparing various studies, revised organizations, new regulations, etc.

Well, that's about all for now. Still don't know when I'll be home, but anticipate around 25 August or before.

Love,
Dan

---

30 July 1969

Dear Folks,

Am winding up my tour and expect to be out of Vietnam in 3–4 weeks, to trade this war for what appears in the news accounts to be open hostilities on a university campus.

You have probably read recently about the incident involving Colonel Rheault, the commander of the Fifth Special Forces Group, and a number of other officers here at headquarters who were relieved of their duties and arrested in connection with the alleged dropping from a helicopter of a VC double agent. This was a real shock to all of us, as I knew Colonel Rheault very well. He came over here for an orientation when he was still commander of the First Special Forces Group on Okinawa, and I was in charge of his briefing and orientation. He seemed like a very straight, decent officer. Major Middleton, the S-2 who was also arrested, is also a very nice guy whom I knew very well. We don't know all of the facts, and they may never be fully known. One rumor is that the agent was actually a triple agent employed also by the South Vietnam government, and the long-standing feud between the Fifth Special Forces Group and the VNSF over the latter's alleged corruption caused the South Vietnam government to blow the whistle. In any case, if our officers did as charged, it would be a very bizarre and unjustifiable act. I can only assume that Colonel Rheault got some really bad advice and, as a newcomer, felt pushed into following it, sort of like President Kennedy and the Bay of Pigs. Speaking of which, this incident became known the same weekend we found out about Teddy Kennedy's accident at Chappaquiddick and Neil Armstrong's walk on the moon—all in all, a newsworthy weekend. Incidentally, the caper with the double agent was run by the S-2 intelligence people, and not by the S-3 operations section which is my group, to my lasting relief.

Colonel Rheault's replacement is Col. Lemberes, who has been with G-3 at USARV and is not even airborne qualified. He is a dynamic and likable individual, but a lot of the Special Forces veterans feel that sending a non-airborne officer to command the Fifth Special Forces Group is an insult and a blatant effort to grind the Group into the dirt. Col. Lemberes immediately sent himself to the nearby Special Forces jump school to remedy his deficiency, and promptly proceeded to break an ankle and make himself unable to serve effectively. It's probably a good time for me to get out of here.

I've had the experience of briefing a number of high-ranking officers and a few civilians while in Nha Trang, particularly incoming division and corps commanders and USARV staff officers. I briefed Gen. Abrams and he was complimentary of the presentation, as I may have mentioned. One time I briefed Adm. [John S.] McCain [Jr.], the Navy Commander-in-Chief in the Pacific (CINC-PAC), who seemed to be as gracious and congenial a gentleman as I have ever met. He has to live each day knowing that his son [John S. McCain III, now a U.S. senator], a navy flier, is a prisoner of war in North Vietnam. I have briefed various media representatives, including Sean Flynn, the son of the late swashbuckling actor Errol Flynn, who apparently sees war reporting as a way of living up to his father's swashbuckling image. I also briefed Maynard Parker and Robert Christopher of *Newsweek*, and spent a lot of time talking privately to Parker at the time of the Col. Rheault incident. The incident itself was off limits, not that I knew anything anyway, but I was allowed and encouraged to give Parker a complete breakdown of Special Forces operations for background purposes.

My friend Marty Green from West Point and Berlin was killed near Ben Het during a Mike Force operation on May 10, which unfortunately was Mother's Day. He was trying to rescue a wounded CIDG while his unit was under heavy NVA machine gun fire. Ben Het is located near the Cambodian border in the northern part of II Corps, where a Special Forces camp was overrun a year ago (one Special Forces officer, a 1LT Leopold, was reportedly captured during the attack). This is also near Dak To, where the 173rd Airborne Brigade was engaged in some major battles in late 1967. Marty's body was not recovered until just the other day. I was visiting Ben Het on another matter, and we brought him back on my helicopter.

Every once in a while you sit back and take a look at this war, at the loss of people like Marty, a bunch of other West Point classmates and friends and a lot of other Americans, and wonder if it is all worthwhile. I think it is. The South Vietnam government may be corrupt (with some exceptions) and authoritarian, but it certainly is better than a communist dictatorship. They may occasionally rough up some opposition politicians and close some opposition newspapers, but at least there are some opposing politicians and newspapers, unlike in Hanoi, Peking, Moscow, etc. We also have to remember that democracy is not ingrained in the people of

Southeast Asia, or much of the undeveloped world, so we cannot expect a perfect democracy in South Vietnam. We also need to remember that South Vietnam is besieged by a massive internal war and that when our own country went through the Civil War Lincoln abolished habeas corpus and imposed a number of other undemocratic restrictions. I also think there is a better chance for long-term democratic improvement if South Vietnam is under U.S. influence and dependent on us for assistance.

One of the major points I make in my briefings of visitors is the efficiency and effectiveness of the USASF role—more bang for the buck, as Col. Aaron always said. We get a lot more VC and NVA casualties at a much lower cost in dollars and U.S. lives than regular U.S. army troop units are able to do. It seems to me we would have been better off limiting our involvement to USASF advisers if we were unwilling to launch a full-scale war over here. The concept of "measured response" or "gradual escalation" simply doesn't seem to work; we either need to go after them with all the resources at our disposal, or give South Vietnam the USASF advisers and supplies and let them try to do it themselves. I gave a briefing recently to Lieutenant Gen. [Fred C.] Weyand, who is Kissinger's military adviser at the Paris peace talks. After the briefing, he invited us all to sit down around him and he talked to us about the peace talks generally. One of the points he made was that the American people seem to be willing to tolerate a war that involves a major cost for a short period of time, or a nominal cost for a prolonged period of time, but are unwilling to tolerate a war which involves a major cost for a prolonged period of time. He and the government seem to realize that this last case is what we find ourselves in, and the best hope for getting out of it is to turn the war back to the Vietnamese, where it belongs, and cut the American cost down to a nominal level.

Well, I've about done my share for this cause, and I can't say things over here are appreciably better than when I arrived. We aren't in the middle of a Tet offensive, the VC have been decimated, and the RVN forces seem to be getting stronger, but the NVA are still pouring down from the North and we've learned not to get too optimistic about progress over here. I just hope that this war doesn't drag on much longer, and that when it does end we remember those who were willing to "bear any burden, pay any price," in JFK's words, to assure the success and survival of liberty in South Vietnam.

I'll call you when I reach the States.

Love,
Dan

EPILOGUE

Looking back, my time in Vietnam was a very intense experience for me, leaving good, bad, bizarre, and even just routine memories that will never be erased. I was fortunate to have made it safely through my nineteen months in Vietnam, departing the country for home in late August 1969. I later became a practicing lawyer in Indianapolis, a husband, and the father of two children.

As my letters reveal, while I was serving in Vietnam I felt frustrated and disillusioned from time to time, particularly over the apparent corruption and aversion to combat of some of my South Vietnamese comrades. I also had doubts that we were making real progress in the war, though we were clearly holding our own and were ultimately victorious in every significant battle fought while the Americans were there. We were simply unable, in the face of the restrictions imposed on us and the eventual loss of domestic political support, to eliminate the VC and NVA and their sympathizers and supply sources. Looking back now, I still believe in our fundamental reasons for involvement, though certainly not all the policies, practices, and strategies we followed in pursuit of our objectives. Whether we could actually have won the war without the restrictions and with continued backing by Congress and with better methods will never be known. I do believe that the outcome of the war was really in the hands of the South Vietnamese government and military, and that it was up to them to demonstrate the superiority of their side to that of the communists, gain the support of their countrymen, and defeat the insurgency and invasion. The

Americans and our other allies could help, but it was ultimately their war to win or lose.

Over the three decades following my departure from Vietnam, I was often very curious about conditions in Vietnam and, especially, in the areas of Ha Tay and Duc Lap. What was the country like under communist rule? What traces, if any, of the bunkers, airstrips, and other physical facilities of my camps remained? Were the villages near my camps still standing, and what did they look like these days? Were there any people remaining in the villages whom I would know, or who would know me, from my comparatively brief time among them? What sort of welcome would I receive, given the long and tortured American presence in that country?

Perhaps more importantly, Vietnam had become a festering emotional sore for me, and I needed to find a way to heal it. This was not because of the war itself or my participation in it; instead, it was due to my personal and defensive reactions to the war protests and to the negative portrayals of our soldiers and veterans that seemed to pervade the media and the arts and entertainment industries. Over the years, these emotion-triggering incidents continually recurred, as each offending article, movie, or other reference to the subject seemed to pick the scab on my sore. It was hard to hear or read the word "Vietnam" without feeling my heart race and my stomach churn. I had reached the point where I, personally, needed to normalize relations with Vietnam and with everything the name connoted. I concluded the best way to start the normalization process would be to see Vietnam firsthand as the functioning country it has now become.

Having decided to return to Vietnam, my wife, Joan, and I worked with a travel company to schedule a tour during January/February 2002 that would take us to the sites of my

**FitzGibbon at the site of his former Special Forces camp at Ha Tay, February 2002.
The camera is facing north from the camp's former airstrip at the bottom of the hill.**
Daniel H. FitzGibbon

former Special Forces camps as well as the usual tourist spots in the country. The trip would overlap the annual Tet celebration, marking the thirty-fourth anniversary of the 1968 Tet Offensive that was in progress during my first visit. The company arranged an itinerary that included stops in Ho Chi Minh City (which out of habit and principle I will persist in calling Saigon), Qui Nhon (the old B-22 HQ and departure point for Ha Tay), Nha Trang (the lovely seaside resort city where Fifth Special Forces Group HQ was located), Buon Ma Thuot (a major city in the Central Highlands, home of the former B-23 HQ when known as Ban Me Thuot, and my gateway to Duc Lap), Hue (the former imperial capital that I had never visited), Hanoi (the capital of French Indochina, North Vietnam, and now all of Vietnam), and the scenic islands of Ha Long Bay.

Flying and driving throughout Vietnam, I was struck once again by the country's natural beauty. Photographs and travel brochures cannot do justice to the majestic coastal mountain ranges; the rich combination of lush green colors in the rice paddies, trees, and other vegetation; and the long and undisturbed sandy beaches. I was pleased to see little evidence of the wartime defoliation and bomb craters that had once scarred portions of the countryside, though defoliation was never as widespread or effective as commonly understood. I actually caught myself identifying ideal ambush sites, concealed approach routes, and impenetrable staging areas, and wondered how we could ever have expected to eliminate a well-supplied guerrilla force in this environment.

Despite the passage of more than three decades and all that had intervened, Vietnam seemed very familiar to me, and I was comfortable and relaxed throughout my trip. The people were very friendly, and small children seeing our facial features often waved and said, "Hello!" As our guides and travel books pointed out, Vietnam had become a country of 80 million people, some 60 percent of whom were not born when the war ended. At one point, during our attempt to locate Ha Tay, we talked with several villagers who were uniformly cordial and helpful, and we were even invited in for tea by a former district chief in the area. My Vietnamese language skills, rusty despite a pre-tour review of my old textbooks, allowed me to handle simple conversations and dealings without an interpreter, and my meager efforts seemed to be appreciated.

The communist government had long since abandoned its collective farms and socialist enterprises in favor of private land ownership, entrepreneurial activity, and stimulation of foreign investment and tourism. This restructuring reversed years of declining production and living standards after the war, and led to economic growth and tangible improvements.

The main reason for my return trip, of course, was to visit the sites of the former Ha Tay and Duc Lap Special Forces camps, but we encountered red (no pun intended) tape in our pursuit of that goal. Vietnam tourism officials had my itinerary at least several weeks, if not months, before my arrival in-country, and my travel company told me I would be able to see both camps. The government's official policy was that foreigners may visit anywhere except military installations, though local police and party officials reportedly impose barriers occasionally out of either ignorance or a desire to extract bribes. The day after I arrived in Vietnam, I was told by our local travel service that the police had barred me from visiting both Ha Tay and Duc Lap because of a joint search for Americans missing in action (MIA). This seemed improbable, since the two locations are 150 miles apart, and further inquiry determined that the joint

U.S./Vietnam MIA team had no searches scheduled for the period of my camp visits. As it turned out, I was able to visit Ha Tay only because of a guide who was willing to proceed without permission, but I was unable to get within twenty miles of Duc Lap. This was a major disappointment to me, but perhaps I will have another opportunity to visit the camp in the future. On the list of historical American disappointments from Vietnam, this one has to rank pretty low.

Our guide met us at the Qui Nhon airport, the former Phu Cat U.S. air force base, and took us by car to Ha Tay with instructions to stay inconspicuous and inside the vehicle. After some false leads and errors in navigation, and repeated stops to consult local villagers, we made it to what unmistakably was my former camp, recognizable despite the lack of buildings and the effect of thirty years' worth of foliage overgrowth. Here, I persuaded my guide that I could freely get out of the car and walk around since there were no houses or villages in sight. The flat surface of the camp's former air strip, with traces of its tar coating, was recognizable despite the growth of trees on the runway. Virtually all the wood, tin, and other materials that had gone into construction of the camp had been removed, presumably by residents of the area for their own use. Even the concrete walls lining our mortar pits and walkways were missing, though the pits and trenches themselves remained as treacherous traps covered by vegetation. During the war, my team had constructed a concrete observation and control tower on the hill in the middle of the camp, but only a few stray pieces of concrete remained where the tower had been.

At Ha Tay I stood on top of the hill and looked in all directions at sights so familiar it was almost as if I had never left. There were the hilltops near my camp where we had positioned security out-posts, the large and thickly forested mountain range to the south and east of camp, the Kim Son River to the north and west that divided the friendly villages near the camp from the hostile village of Vinh Hoa across the river, the rice paddies to the west where I had launched my first combat operation, and the 506 valley to the southeast where my most intense and difficult battles had taken place. The villages were almost hidden from view now, thanks to new and larger trees surrounding them. I paused for a few minutes to reflect on my eight months there and the people I had known and worked with during that period. I was thankful so many of us had made it out safely and remembered with sadness those who had not. I wished the villagers now living in the area health, happiness, and prosperity.

At the bottom of the hill, on the road to the villages to the north, there was a monument dated April 9, 1972, with the name Go Loi. There was also a large and well-decorated NVA cemetery nearby. I learned that the people in the vicinity referred to the site of my camp as Go Loi, rather than Ha Tay or the names of nearby villages shown on the map. There had obviously been a large battle on that site and date, which was three years after my camp's CIDG were converted to regional militia. I later determined that the NVA Eastertide Offensive of 1972, which had focused primarily on northern South Vietnam, Kontum in the Central Highlands, and An Loc northwest of Saigon, had also included significant fighting between the NVA Third Division and the ARVN Twenty-second Division in the region around Ha Tay.

After leaving my camp, I asked the guide to drive us along Highway 506, now as then a dirt road in a valley with rice paddies on either side and steep, densely wooded mountains just beyond. I thought of the violence, destruction, and fear that had marked this valley during my earlier stay, and took great comfort in the thriving rice paddies and peaceful scenery now evident all around me.

Schoolhouse constructed in 1968 by the Ha Tay Special Forces camp detachment, A-227, as it appeared in February 2002.
Daniel H. FitzGibbon

Returning to the main road leading northeast from Ha Tay to Bong Son, we passed the villages where my team and I had made frequent visits to cement relationships with village elders, provide medical and hygiene assistance, and set up occasional night ambushes along approaches to the villages. I regretted that I was unable to get out and walk around the villages, but I understood my guide's unwillingness for me to do so given the risks he had already taken on my behalf. I later realized that visiting the villages would undoubtedly have proved disappointing, and that I had been vain and naive to have thought otherwise. While my eight months' service there meant a great deal to my life, it would have been a brief and inconsequential moment to a generation of people who had endured so much fighting, deprivation, and change over so many years.

As we drove past the villages, however, I saw one building that caught my eye and brought us to a quick stop. It was a small concrete schoolhouse for primary age children, constructed under the supervision of my A team in 1968 as the first school in the district. At the time it was built it was the cause of considerable excitement in the area. The dedication ceremony was attended by numerous ranking South Vietnamese and American civilian and military leaders and was featured in a photo spread in the Fifth Special Forces Group magazine. It was unclear from the road whether the schoolhouse was still used as such, since there were no signs to mark its function, but at least it stood as silent testimony to our efforts on behalf of the people there.

It was gratifying to see that progress had come to the villages around Ha Tay. Instead of huts with bamboo or clay walls and thatched roofs, most of the residents lived in concrete houses with clay tile or tin roofs. Electricity wires and poles lined Highway 506 and the road to Bong Son, and most houses were topped with television antennas. The people in the fields and villages appeared to be fed and clothed reasonably well, wearing western-style apparel rather than the old black pajamas, though the farmers still used the old manual methods to work their rice paddies. There were quite a few new buildings in the area, most of them government or communist-party facilities. Perhaps the most rewarding sights were the numerous schools in the area—buildings that were far larger and nicer than the schoolhouse my team constructed, accommodating not only primary grades but also high school students. We were told repeatedly of the high literacy rate among the people of Vietnam these days, and certainly the abundance of schools would seem to support that claim.

As we proceeded back to Highway One and Qui Nhon, I wondered if my time in Vietnam in 1968–69 had been as meaningless as the empty pits and trenches on the site of the former Ha Tay camp. Then, I thought about the schoolhouse we had built and realized that it had produced part of a new generation of educated citizens and perhaps laid the foundation for the other schools that followed. I considered our small role in the effort to block an expansionist communist system and realized the local society was flourishing under capitalism and that communism had receded, not expanded, in the world. I took note of the young Vietnamese who had completed their educations, and of the neighboring countries that had developed and prospered during the war while I and more than two million Americans who served in Vietnam bought them vital time to mature and succeed. Finally, I recalled that I had volunteered for Vietnam, and for my duty as an A team leader, to help the people of that country, and realized with pleasure that the people there are doing well. I concluded that our service and sacrifices did have meaning and our efforts were not entirely in vain.

I didn't neutralize all of my emotions associated with Vietnam, and perhaps I never will. I still get agitated when I read some comment that, in my view, misstates or distorts what we did in the war and why we fought it. But now when I see the word "Vietnam," I don't think first of a war or a source of national division and discord; I think of a real and vibrant country.

GLOSSARY

People

My letters refer to various people by name, most of them identified when mentioned or identifiable in the context. My family
members, mentioned occasionally, included in addition to my
parents an older sister, Sally, and her husband, Linc, and children, Sean and Tracy; another older sister, Julie, and her children, Doug, Dawn, Dana, and Darren, who lived with my parents at the time; and a younger sister, Nancy, who married her
husband, Don, early in my Vietnam tour and went off on a
Mennonite mission to Algeria. I was still a bachelor and would
remain one for five more years. There are also references to
Uncle Larry, one of my father's brothers; Nels Marin, Bob Mack,
and Marty Green, friends and fellow officers I knew in Berlin
(and, in Marty's case, at West Point); Orphie Bridges, an Arvin
Industries executive; Skip Lindeman, a friend from high school;
and Max Andress, my high school football coach.

Terms

A camp: The base for Civilian Irregular Defense
                 Group forces led by a Vietnamese Special
                 Forces A Team, which in turn was advised by a
                 U.S. Army Special Forces A team.

A team: The basic unit of Special Forces; three officers
                 and ten experienced non-commissioned officers.

A-227:   The A team based at Ha Tay, Binh Dinh
               Province, South Vietnam; also known as
               Detachment A-227.

A-239:   The A team based at Duc Lap, Quang Duc
               Province, South Vietnam; also known as
               Detachment A-239.

APC: Armored Personnel Carrier; a track mounted
               vehicle that carries eleven troops.

ARVN: Army of the Republic of Vietnam (South
               Vietnam).

B team: The control unit for two or more Special
               Forces A teams.

B-22:   The B team based in Qui Nhon, Binh Dinh
               Province, South Vietnam, that controlled
               Detachment A-227 at Ha Tay, among other
               units; also called Detachment B-22.

B-23:   The B team based in Ban Me Thuot, Darlac
               Province, South Vietnam, that controlled
               Detachment A-239 at Duc Lap, among other
               units; also called Detachment B-23.

C team: The control unit for two or more Special
               Forces B teams.

C-2:	The C team based in Pleiku, Pleiku Province, South Vietnam, that controlled B-22 and B-23, among other units; also called Detachment C-2.
CA/PO:	Civil Affairs/Psychological Operations.
Charlie:	American slang for the Vietcong communist forces.
CIDG:	Civilian Irregular Defense Group; indigenous forces based at Special Forces A camps.
Claymore:	Electrical or fuse-detonated above-ground mine that, when detonated, sends small steel pellets in a forward arc.
CO:	Commanding Officer.
Company B:	Another designation for C-2.
Concertina:	Circular barbed wire that stretches out or contracts like an accordion.
Draw:	A shallow gully or ravine.
Duc Lap:	Location of a Special Forces A camp in Quang Duc Province, South Vietnam, near the Cambodian border.
Duster:	A track-mounted vehicle with guns that fire 40 mm grenades in rapid automatic fire.

FAC: Forward Air Controller; a U.S. Air Force pilot
                     flying a light plane and coordinating/directing
                     tactical air and artillery strikes.

Fougasse: Barrels of gasoline, oil, naphtha, and C-4
                     plastic explosive rigged for detonation,
                     usually electronically.

Fifth Special   The primary U.S. Army Special Forces unit in
Forces Group: South Vietnam that controlled C-2/Company
                     B, among other units; headquartered in Nha
                     Trang, Khanh Hoa Province, South Vietnam.

1LT: First Lieutenant.

Free Fire Zone: Area where South Vietnamese officials had
                     declared no civilians could live or work and
                     where all persons were presumed to be VC
                     and could be taken under fire by artillery
                     and air strikes.

GI: American soldier; "government issue."

Ha Tay: Location of a Special Forces A camp in Binh
                     Dinh Province, South Vietnam, near the
                     South China Sea.

HQ: Headquarters.

LLDB: Luc Luong Dac Biet, the local term for
                     Vietnamese Special Forces.

LON:	Location Overnight; place in the field where a unit stops for the night.
LRRP:	Long Range Reconnaissance Patrol.
LSAT:	Law School Admission Test.
LZ:	Landing Zone.
MACV:	Military Assistance Command, Vietnam; the unit providing advisers to South Vietnamese military forces.
Montagnard:	French name for indigenous nomadic tribes living in the Central Highlands of South Vietnam and elsewhere in Southeast Asia.
NCO:	Non-Commissioned Officer; enlisted man ranked sergeant E-5 or higher.
NVA:	North Vietnamese Army; communist forces infiltrated from North Vietnam.
PX:	Post Exchange; store for American military personnel.
R & R:	Rest and Recuperation; typically, a seven-day leave to one of several designated locations outside Vietnam.

RF/PF:
Regional Forces/Popular Forces; civilian militia under control of the provincial (RF) or district (PF) chief.

ROK:
Republic of Korea; South Korean armed forces.

RP:
Registration Point; location of a pre-set target for an artillery piece or mortar.

RVN:
Republic of Vietnam; South Vietnam.

Special Forces:
Army special operations unit that typically engages in unconventional warfare, advising or directing much larger units of indigenous troops; U.S. Army Special Forces soldiers are nicknamed "Green Berets" for their distinctive headgear.

TAOR:
Tactical Area of Operational Responsibility; geographic area around an A camp in which CIDG and Special Forces are expected to conduct ground patrols and other operations and provide security, civil affairs, medical hygiene, and other assistance to civilians.

TOC:
Tactical Operations Center; place within an A camp where the American A team has its main communications and other command and control equipment; the A team's headquarters.

II Corps:	Military district in north central South Vietnam, one of four in the country.
USAF:	U.S. Air Force.
USARV:	U.S. Army, Vietnam; unit containing all American army troops and units.
USASF:	U.S. Army Special Forces.
VC:	Vietcong; communist forces indigenous to South Vietnam.
VN:	Vietnam.
VNSF:	Vietnamese Special Forces (South Vietnam).
XO:	Executive officer; second in command of a unit.